OUT OF BOUNDS

FROM BROKEN NBA DREAMS TO REDEMPTION

THE CHRIS WASHBURN STORY

CHRIS WASHBURN
AND RON CHEPESIUK

WILDBLUE
PRESS

WildBluePress.com

OUT OF BOUNDS published by:
WILDBLUE PRESS
P.O. Box 102440
Denver, Colorado 80250

Publisher Disclaimer: Any opinions, statements of fact or fiction, descriptions, dialogue, and citations found in this book were provided by the author, and are solely those of the author. The publisher makes no claim as to their veracity or accuracy, and assumes no liability for the content.

ISBN 978-1-964730-46-2 Hardcover
ISBN 978-1-964730-47-9 Trade Paperback
ISBN 978-1-964730-48-6 eBook
Cover design © 2025 WildBlue Press. All rights reserved.

Interior Formatting and Book Cover Design by Elijah Toten
www.totencreative.com

OUT OF BOUNDS

"Fall Seven Times, Stand Up Eight"

– Japanese Proverb

CONTENTS

FOREWORD
By Chuckie Brown*

I can remember in high school being recruited by North Carolina State University, and the coach who was recruiting me, Tommy Abatemarco, saying, "I can't believe what I am seeing! Such power and grace at the same time and so dominant amongst the best players in the country." He was talking about Chris Washburn.

I called Tommy back and said I would love to play with Chris Washburn! I ended up committing to NC State and having the opportunity to play with Chris. It was an incredible experience. I also got to see him behind the scenes and the type of person he is.

Chris has a very big heart, is very approachable and is very humble. He would let me borrow his car and never asked where I was going, and I saw him do that with other players as well. Chris was so talented I thought basketball was easy for him. I can remember practices where he dominated a Greek player, who was on the Greek national team named Panagiotis Fasoulas. Coach V brought him in specifically to be able to push Wash a little bit in practice, but Wash would destroy him every day.

Seeing Wash get drafted third overall and him coming back to campus really made us proud to know him and to see that he had never forgotten us. Wash inspired me to want to make it to the NBA, I always remembered him playing against the best players in the country, and he would be the best player on the floor. We beat Kentucky when they were number one in the country, and they had the great Kenny Sky Walker. We smacked UNC (University of North Carolina), and they had Brad Daugherty. We were the last team to beat Louisville University, and they went on to win the national championship with Never Nervous Pervis Ellison.

In all those games, Wash dominated and put himself on the map! I have known Chris for years, and I have been able to see him grow as a person, even though he has had his troubles with substance abuse. He has never changed from being the kind-hearted person he is.

I can remember seeing him come to the gym when he was in the John Lucas rehabilitation center, and I was impressed how all of the guys who were playing with the Houston Rockets knew him and respected him. That said a lot about the player he was. I have talked to Chris, and I can remember him telling me about his son Julian, who was playing at UTEP (the University of Texas El Paso). I know that even, given his struggles, he had tried to be a great father to his children.

Seeing Chris now and the things he is trying to do is very inspiring. He knows he made mistakes, but he also knows that he can help someone who is heading down the wrong road.

Chucky Brown is a legendary North Carolina State player (1985-89), who played for twelve different NBA teams (1989-2002), a record he shared at one time with four other players.

PROLOGUE

SUDDEN DEATH

"… I never left the room. I never went to the class. I missed all of my exams. I just sat in my room for hours. My only thought was: where can I get more of that stuff without people knowing."

In January of 1986, Chris Washburn and Len Bias were two of the best players in college basketball. With his amazing leaping ability and imposing physical stature (6'8" and 220 pounds), Bias, a senior, was dynamic, exciting, a surefire superstar when he turned pro later that year.

A shade under seven feet in height, Chris Washburn, a sophomore at North Carolina State University, was also a gifted athlete, a can't-miss future pro who combined soft hands with power.

In early 1986, the two athletes met, and their lives changed dramatically.

CHRIS WASHBURN: "I first met Len Bias when our team went to College Park, Maryland, to play for the University of Maryland Terrapins. I'm one of those guys who have never really followed sports. But I did see a highlight of Len on TV, and I said to myself: 'That boy can play!' I was impressed.

"Before the game, me and some of my teammates walked the halls at the University of Maryland when I bumped into Len. It was a short, friendly conversation. We said we would see each other at the game. That night, they won the game, but I could see why Len was an All-American. He was spectacular.

"The next time we met was in March (1986) when Len's team came to Raleigh to play us. We lost in a real nail biter by one point. Len and I shook hands after the game and went our way. The season for us ended when we lost to Kansas University in the Elite 8 of the NCAA basketball tournament.

"I was in my dorm room one night, getting ready for an exam early next morning, when I got a knock on the door. It was Charles Logan, a friend of mine, whom we nicknamed Lo-C. He was with Lorenzo Charles, who played on the Wolfpack with me and whom we called C-Lo. Charles asked if I had anybody in the room with me. I said no. He said that he'd be back. He wanted somebody for me to meet. A little later, Charles returned with Len Bias.

"I said to Len, 'Man, what are you doing here.' I was excited. I looked up to Len.

I wanted to be on his level.

Len said he was in North Carolina for the bomb storming. (In basketball, bomb storming is when teams or athletes travel to different locations to play exhibition matches. Bomb-storming teams are different from traveling teams because they don't operate within an established league.)

"Len was carrying a glass jar with him. I thought it was weird, but I didn't pay it any mind. I had an exam early the next morning at 7:50. I was tired, but hey, Len Bias is here. I went to the bathroom and came back. They had taken what looked like a rock from the jar. I found out later it was crack cocaine. I had no experience with the drug. The only drug I had taken up to that time was weed.

"So, C-Lo lights up a crack cigarette and asks me if I wanted to try it. I declined. They kept smoking among themselves. They kept asking me if I wanted some, but I kept refusing. I told them I had class early that morning, and it was getting late.

"A couple of hours passed. It was getting light outside. I needed to get ready for class. I went and showered and came out of the bathroom. They were still smoking crack. They kept asking me if I wanted to try it. Finally, I relented and said I would give it a try.

"I took a hit. It was my first time. Wow! It was one of the best feelings I've ever had. My heart started to beat a little faster. I got a little sweat on my forehead.

"I was dead tired before I took a hit. Now I was wide awake.

"It was around 7 am. My class, remember, was at 7:50. But I never left the room. I never went to the class. I missed all of my exams. I just sat in my room for hours. My only thought was: where can I get more of that stuff without people knowing.

"A week later, Coach Jim Valvano told me that I had missed my exams and so was ineligible to play basketball the next season. Man, my life had changed."

But so did Len Bias's. A few months later, Len Bias was found unconscious in a dormitory room on the University of Maryland campus. He was rushed to the hospital but died of cardiac arrhythmia related to a cocaine overdose.

CHRIS WASHBURN: "I was shocked by Len's death. It scared me, but it didn't stop me from abusing crack cocaine."

1

ROOTS

*"I would read all this stuff about me. They talked
about my poor academic performance and how
I was struggling in school, how my grades were
terrible. I would say to myself: 'who is that dummy?'
I didn't recognize him."* ~ Chris Washburn

Chris Washburn grew up not knowing who his birth parents were. He was born to twenty-five-year-old Ruby McClendon on May 13, 1966. Miss Ruby, as she is referred to, was in a relationship with a man whom she did not know was married. When he found out Miss Ruby was pregnant with Chris, he demanded she get an abortion.

RUBY MCCLENDON: "Many men don't like to stick around when they learn their woman is pregnant. I already had a son. I was having health problems with boils. I was not making too much money at work. The responsibility of supporting another child was just too much for me. I contacted an adoption agency, which said it would find a fine family for my child. I gave him up. I cried over it. It was the hardest thing I ever had to do."

Today, Chris Washburn, the child who was adopted, has a theory about his birth and the drug addiction that came to plague him later in his life.

CHRIS WASHBURN: "My biological mom has a son, Michael, and he was raised as a single child like me. My biological mom was in poor health and that's why she put me up for adoption. Back in the 60s, an unmarried woman with two kids wasn't looked upon as being right, so she had to get rid of one of the kids, and that was me.

My brother was raised as a single child. I was raised as a single child. My dad has a daughter who was raised as a single child. Nobody knew each other. I didn't know Michael. Michael didn't know her. But we all ended up having crack cocaine problems. All of us went through rehab. I'm thinking our problem, the problem that I had later in life, may be genetic-related."

With his adoption, Chris Washburn's life started off on the right track. He was adopted by Dwight and Savannah Washburn from Hickory, North Carolina, a small hamlet located about ninety-eight miles from Greensboro. They changed Chris's name to Christopher Scott Washburn. Chris fondly recalls his great childhood.

CHRIS WASHBURN: "I was fortunate to have parents that wanted a child.

My mom was thirty-six and father was five years older than my mom. She was unable to have children, so when she finally adopted me, she was thirty-six years old. They were financially ready for a child.

"I can remember when I was really young, about three or four years old. It was Christmas, and I was showered with presents. I got expensive gifts like electric cars and all kinds of TV games when they first came out. I thought everybody got things like that. I didn't know that a lot of families couldn't afford them. I guess I was fortunate to be an only child."

However, all of his childhood experiences were not pleasant for Washburn. Being bigger and easygoing, he was often picked on and bullied by other youngsters. His mother told him to pay the aggressors no mind, just walk away.

CHRIS WASHBURN: "My mom told me I was bigger than the kids, and if I fought back, I could hurt someone. So, when I did decide to defend myself, I never really tried to fight back. I would always hold back my punches. I would block all the blows, but never hit back. They'd be punching, and I'd be blocking."

On one occasion, Chris was chased right into his home by a bully, and his mother saw first-hand what her son was experiencing. Savannah confronted the bully and chased him out of the house. The bully's parents came to the house and confronted Chris's mom. It was the first time Chris saw his mom get into a fight.

A couple of weeks after the incident, Savannah put Chris in karate class. She was not going to be around him all the time, so Mama Washburn decided that her son was just going to have to learn how to take care of himself.

Al Young, a close friend of Chris lived about a hundred yards away from the Wallace family. He recalls the first time he saw Chris.

AL YOUNG: "I was walking along when I saw this big kid standing by a car. He was so much bigger than any of us kids…. much bigger than me, even though I was four years older than him. I introduced myself to Chris. We hit it off. We've been close ever since. Chris is a very likeable, good guy."

In the fourth grade, Washburn was diagnosed with a learning disability. He always struggled in school because of it, although many people did not know about his disability. His poor academic background in high school would later follow him into his basketball-playing days at North Carolina State University.

CHRIS WASHBURN: "I would read all this stuff about me. They talked about my poor academic performance and how I was struggling in school, how my grades were terrible. I would say to myself: 'who is that dummy?' I didn't recognize him."

By the summer of 1977, when Chris was in the sixth grade, his size kept the bullies away. He had grown to six feet in height and weighed 230 pounds. Chris loved football, but being so much bigger than the other kids, his mom had to carry a birth certificate when she attended games to prove her son was as old and as young as she said he was.

When Chris entered junior high, he had grown another seven inches. With his increased size, Chris's clothes became an issue. He was simply outgrowing them too quickly. But Washburn was fast becoming quite the athlete. He was big but also quick and strong. He was playing football and excelled at it.

Al Young also starred in football, basketball, and track at Hickory High School. He would later be a seventh-round pick out of Virginia Tech in the 1985 NBA Draft.

AL YOUNG: "Chris's mother got me to teach him how to pass, run and punt. He never played high school football. He played recreational football. They literally had to change the rules of the game for him. He was a running back, a huge running back. He would get the ball and literally carry several players across the goal line with him."

Washburn did enjoy football. Basketball, however, was another story.

CHRIS WASHBURN: "I really enjoyed basketball, and I was getting good at it. People started to come to my games simply to see me play. In the seventh grade, I dunked the ball for the first time. The following year, I was scoring thirty points a game and grabbing close to fifteen rebounds a game. I was getting better and better and having fun."

Chris Washburn was a marvel on the basketball court. He was extremely coordinated and could dribble, despite being a big man. He was huge, a boy in a man's body, even though he never lifted weights.

One night, Savannah Washburn came to realize how exceptional a basketball player her son was when she attended a banquet. She later recalled: "I went to a team banquet, and the speaker was the athletic director at Lenoir Rhyne (a small college in western North Carolina). He gave a speech and at the end he turned to Chris and said: 'You're a coach's dream, Chris. You're a franchise.'"

The athletic director calling her son a "franchise," rather than pleasing Savannah, scared her. Here was her son, an eighth grader, and at 6'11, much bigger than kids his age and the man was calling him a franchise. She realized her son may look like a man but inside that big body was her little boy.

As Washburn's popularity as a basketball player grew, he began to see how he was treated differently. Washburn was a young boy, but he began recognizing his athletic ability was opening doors for him.

CHRIS WASHBURN: "People I didn't even know were paying for my meals. I could get into clubs when I was still too young. People would come up and praise me. I would read the newspapers and see all the praise they heaped on me. Yeah, it was heady."

David Craft, who coached Washburn's freshman and sophomore years at Hickory High School, later recalled for the *Seattle Times* newspaper Washburn's size as a grammar schooler and his talent as a basketballer. "I've never seen anybody with the talent he has," Craft told the newspaper. "He was big, but he never went through the awkward stage. As a freshman and sophomore, he played like a senior. Chris started on the varsity when he was a freshman, and he scored 21 points in his first game."

By the time Chris was thirteen, his parents were ready to send him to basketball camp. There are several excellent basketball camps in the U.S. His parents chose the one closest to them at Gardner Webb. About 46 miles from Hickory, the basketball camp at Gardner-Webb University describes itself as "an intensive and high-expectation basketball camp that helps train athletes to become stronger players and better leaders." For the first time, Chris was able to test himself against other talented athletes outside his hometown area.

He was excited about the experience and saw that he could compete.

Given his basketball prowess, Washburn was able to get into the prestigious Five-Star basketball camp in Pennsylvania. Today, the camp can boast a fifty-five-year tradition with 250, 000 alumna, 500 NBA players, and 10,000 Division 1 players in its history. The luminaries who have worked out or taught at 5 Star include Michael Jordan, Steve Curry, Lebron James, Isiah Thomas, Patrick Ewing, and Chris Mullins, among others.

CHRIS WASHBURN: "By my 7th and 8th grades, people were talking to me about going to basketball camps. I had never heard anything about basketball camps. With my mom's permission, I went to the one in PA. It was the first time I had actually been away from home and the first time on a plane. So, I was a little nervous.

"I was only fifteen years old but looked older, like a young man in college.

Because it was my first time at the camp, they put me on the lowest level. There were three levels, with the top one called the NBA. By the evening of my first day at the camp, I was playing at the NBA level.

"People couldn't believe this little kid was playing against seniors and doing quite well. I was playing so well, in fact, that I made the all-star team. But, unfortunately back then, Mr. Garfinkel, who ran the camp, would only let seniors play in a game. He explained to me that he didn't want me to go out and do well, and maybe cost some of the seniors a scholarship. So, I had to sit on the bench. I was happy that I made the top level but unhappy that I could not play."

When Washburn returned home, his basketball experience was totally different for him. He was playing with the varsity now. One had to come to Washburn's games early, or you did not get in because the stands had filled up.

CHRIS WASHBURN: "My scoring average was turning heads. College coaches started coming to see me play. We started bringing recognition to our hometown, and we were invited to a couple tournaments in Greensboro that we won.

"I noticed I was starting to get some special treatment. I would do little things that got me in trouble, but I would get away with them. I think that, if I had been told no early on in my life, I would not have experienced some of the pitfalls I later had in life."

By age 15, Washburn was starting to get letters from colleges, lots of them. He also got letters from two NBA teams: the Boston Celtics and Washington Wizards. Washburn wondered how they knew about him. The inquiries were validation for him. He knew he could play the game.

When Chris came back from camp he had grown to 6' 7". His mother was concerned about his growth spurt and took him to the doctor to find out if there was anything wrong with him.

CHRIS WASHBURN: "The doctor told my mom that there was nothing wrong with me. He said that I was in good shape and that all my bones looked good. But it was getting costly for my family. Every time she bought clothes, within three or four days they would be too short for me. There were no stores for big people my size. So, for a while I had to walk around with pants that were too short."

While Washburn's basketball was progressing tremendously, he struggled with his academic studies. His grades were poor in high school, his academic record, erratic. The records showed that in his first two years at Hickory High School, he earned mostly Ds and Fs. At Fork Union Military Academy in Virginia, where he spent his junior year, he earned Cs, Ds and Fs. He knew he would have to take the SAT. None of that bothered him though.

He later recalled after getting into college: "The coaches over there told me: 'You already signed, you're already in school, you just have to take the test to get into college.' They told me it didn't matter what score I was getting. I went in for about twenty-two minutes, and I just marked down [answers] … mark, mark, mark. If the coach told me I needed 700, 800 on the test to get into school, I could've got that. But when they said I didn't need it, I didn't need it."

Washburn achieved a 470, a score that only narrowly exceeded the minimum requirement. Later, news reports about his poor SAT score would help spur the NCAA plans to update its criteria for athlete eligibility in higher education.[1]

Washburn's parents decided that acquiring some discipline might help their son. So, they enrolled him in an academy. They chose Fork Union Military Academy in Fork Union, Virginia, an 800-student all-boy's school for grades 7 to 12. Fork Union is about a five-hour drive from Hickory. The school boasts that 100 percent of its graduating seniors have received college acceptance.

Todd Black, from Virginia Beach, Virginia, was Chris's roommate at the school.

TODD BLACK: "Fork Union was a military school. I wouldn't say it was like West Point, but the institute was highly structured and regimented. It had rules and regulations for everything. We had to put on these big red helmets and carry a gun and march for an hour. I didn't get many demerits. Maybe twenty to forty. Chris, on the other hand, accumulated demerits to the point where he was a few short of being expelled from the school.

CHRIS WASHBURN: "You could get 150 demerits before you were expelled from the school. I reached 145, and I got them before basketball season started. They were for petty things like walking across the grass. It was a military school, and they had rank. I didn't like it when a younger kid with rank over me tried to order me around. I would argue and get demerits. It was tough. I had to go to class, so I had to do the punishment in my free time."

---

1. Marc J. Spears, "Washburn Traveled Long Road to Recovery," Yahoo! Sports, July 15, 2010, https://sports.yahoo.com/mc-washburn-life071510.html.

Arritt, a student from Fayetteville, West Virginia, decided to spend an extra year at Fork Union Military Academy after high school. During that year, he was a leader on the basketball team and also competed in track. After finishing at Fork Union in 1960, he went to the University of Virginia where he played basketball and participated in track and cross country for four years.

In 1966, Arritt came back to Fork Union as a teacher and coach. He taught biology and coached basketball, track, and a younger football team. He started as an assistant basketball coach but was promoted to lead the postgraduate basketball team in 1971.

More than 500 of Arritt's players have been sent to college ranks. Seven of his players have been sent to the NBA and nearly 25 former players have taught at the high school or college level. The Academy has produced more than 117 NFL players. Eddie George, who played running back in the NFL for nine seasons after winning the Heisman trophy in 1995, Anthony Castonzo, former offensive tackle for the Indianapolis Colts and Mel Turpin, former University of Kentucky and NBA player, are three of the school's most prominent alumni. Arritt passed away on June 16, 2021, at age 79.

In an interview with the Raleigh *News and Observer* on January 28, 1985, Arritt said he found Washburn to be "playful and mischievous" away from the court but said Washburn had a "calm year" and no run-ins with the law.

While stating that Chris went to class, Arritt revealed that Washburn did get some demerits. "All cadets do," Arritt said. "There was one time we were playing New York's Riverside JC. We had a lot of our players' parents staying at the motel, and Chris and some other players were caught breaking curfew and being away from the barracks. That gave Chris too many demerits, a lot of our kids do, and he had to walk them off before being allowed to rejoin the team."

Black credits Fork Union coach Fletcher Arritt with helping to keep him, Chris and his fellow players in line.

TODD BLACK: "Coach Arritt was no nonsense type of coach. We players knew that if we got too far out of line, he wouldn't hesitate to kick us off the team."

Washburn says coach Arritt had a positive impact on him and his development.

CHRIS WASHBURN: "He just made sure that I did the things that I needed to do. He was a good coach. He helped turn me into a basketball player. At the time, I didn't know how bad a shape I was in until I got to Fork Union. By the time I left, I was in the best shape I've ever been as far as being an athlete."

Washburn enjoyed playing for coach Arritt.

CHRIS WASHBURN: "I was sixteen years old and playing against boys who were older than me, some as old 20 years old. I won the MVP, and at that young age, I was ranked in the top 100 players in the country. I was turning a lot of heads. I was having a lot of fun."

Black states Washburn was definitely the best basketball player with whom he has played.

TODD BLACK: "During his junior and senior years in high school, he was ranked the number one player in the country. He was nearly seven feet tall, but he had the skills of a 6' 5" player. His talent level was off the charts. He was a team player. He didn't hog the ball. The game wasn't about him."

Playing at Fork Union turned out to be a profitable experience as well. He started to receive envelopes stuffed with money, thousands of dollars. The money was given anonymously, put on the desk in his room when Chris was out, or sent anonymously through the mail.

Black recalls that he would get perhaps four or five recruiting letters from colleges every month. Washburn, on the other hand, would get more than a dozen in a week.

TODD BLACK: "If a coach really wanted you, he would send you a hand written note. I would get the odd one. Chris would get several of them a week.

He would get a handwritten note in a thick envelope stuffed with twenty-dollar bills. Chris would laugh about it and put the money in his footlocker. I bet he had $10,000 to $30,000 in his footlocker, money he received from different schools."

CHRIS WASHBURN: "I never knew where the money came from, but it really helped out my family. We weren't poor, but we weren't rich either. I didn't see anything wrong with taking it."

By the time Washburn was at Fork Union, his high school junior year, he was perhaps the country's most highly regarded high school player. After graduating from high school in 1984, he became a three-time *Parade* All-American. He and Danny Manning from Kansas University headed a list of forty high school players named to the *Parade* All-America team. The 28th annual team was selected in collaboration with a nationwide panel of college coaches, scouts, and recruiters. Only two other high-school centers besides Washburn were three-time All-Americans – Lew Alcindor and Ralph Sampson. Washburn made an impressive 79 percent of his field-goal attempts his last year as a high school All-American.

Washburn went to summer school in 1984 with the idea of making a decision on where he wanted to go to college. His plans had now changed dramatically.

CHRIS WASHBURN: "For my senior year, I wanted to go back to Fork Union. I had made friends there and enjoyed the atmosphere. I had gotten to know the coach, and I liked him. I knew what to expect from the school. Then I got a letter from the school, saying that I could not attend there because I had signed a letter of intent to go to North Carolina State University. The notification came from the school and not the coach. I couldn't go back there. It put me in a bind. It was the fall, and most of the other schools had already started classes. So, at the least, if I could get into another school, I would be behind with my schoolwork. But my mom looked and looked. Finally, she found a school willing to take me in at the late date."

The high school Chris's family chose was the Laurinburg Institute in Laurinburg, North Carolina, a small city about a two-and-a-half-hour drive from Hickory. Later *Sports Illustrated* magazine would report that Washburn had been counseled on the transfers by NC State Wolfpack coaches. Valvano would later deny that report and claimed Washburn left because he was "unhappy at Fork Union."

Laurinburg is a historic African American preparatory school founded by Emmanuel Monty and Tinny McDuffie at the request of Booker T. Washington. Today, it offers education in grades nine to twelve. Bishop McDuffie, the grandson, is the school's headmaster.

Laurinburg is now the only Black institution of its kind in the United States. The school is noted for its output of highly accomplished alumni. It includes a rich basketball tradition, having produced several All Americans, collegiate players, international players, and NBA players. Notable alumni include several NBA players, such as Charlie Davis, Jimmy Walker, and Charlie Scott. Noted jazz musician Dizzy Gillespie is also an alumnus.

BISHOP MCDUFFIE: "Was Chris Washburn the best player ever at Laurinburg? We're talking about a lot of great players. Let's just say he was one of the best."

According to a posting on the school's website, the Institute's basketball program is designed to "improve the total level of fitness of athletes by developing strength, agility, speed, and endurance." The web page notes that, according to Joseph Milford in the December 2, 2014, edition of *Elite Daily*, "Laurinburg Institute is number five of ten high schools that have produced the most NBA players in history."

CHRIS WASHBURN: "I essentially went to Laurinburg because it was October, a late date for registering for high school, and it was the last high school to accept applications. My mom sent me to Oak Hill Academy (located in Mouth of Wilson, Virginia). I didn't like it there, so after a couple of days I called my parents and said I wanted to come home. They refused, so I said, 'If you don't come and get me, I will walk home.' They relented and took me out of the school.

Laurinburg was the only all black school of its kind in the country. It was the first time I was in a situation where there were no whites. I was with my own. I felt comfortable"

Chris met basketball coach Bishop McDuffie and the two hit it off.

CHRIS WASHBURN: "Coach McDuffie is one of the coolest guys I know. I'm friends with him 'til this day."

McDuffie said his school had no problems with Washburn during his stay there.

BISHOP MCDUFFIE: "There were no issues. Later they portrayed him as the face of the troubled athlete. But he fit in well at our school."

At the time, school officials claimed that Chris's athletic talent had nothing to do with his admission to Laurinburg.

BISHOP MCDUFFIE: "We didn't know there was a Chris Washburn. His mother called, and what she described about him made him sound like any other normal young boy. We didn't know he had the skills or the height he has until he showed up."

Washburn's grades improved at Laurinburg. He earned Bs and Cs. "Those grades pushed Washburn's overall high school grade-point average up to a C or 2.0. The NCAA requires athletes to have a 2.0 average in high school to be eligible to play college sports."[2]

Washburn liked the social environment Laurinburg offered.

CHRIS WASHBURN: "I could smell marijuana in the air. It was different than at Fork Union. Weed wasn't available there. We had movie night. Me and some of the boys would sneak out of a movie and go into the woods where we would meet some city boys and drink beer and do weed. I would walk the mile or so back to the school and be at the movie before it ended."

Laurinburg wasn't the first time Washburn had smoked weed.

CHRIS WASHBURN: "The earliest I had smoked weed was in the tenth grade. My uncles and cousins would come by the house, sit on the porch and smoke a joint. They'd

2. "N.C. St. Took Washburn despite Low SAT Score," Los Angeles Times, February 9, 1985, https://www.latimes.com/archives/la-xpm-1985-02-09-sp-4192-story.html.

light up and say, 'Here you want to try it.' I'd say, 'Yeah, give me a hit.' They'd say, 'Okay, but don't tell your mama.'

"When I'm smoking weed, everything is funny to me. I'd be walking and somebody would pass me by. They'd stare at me, and I would start laughing.

Couldn't help myself. Everybody around me knew I was on to something, except my mamma (chuckles)."

Washburn would smoke marijuana, but it did not affect his play. On December 27, 1983, Chris Washburn totaled 18 points, 16 rebounds, six blocks, and two assists as Laurinburg, his school, fell to Ben Franklin, 83-69. After the game, the crowd in attendance was abuzz. Everyone was asking: how good is Chris Washburn?

"I heard he was the best player in the country . . . and I agree," Franklin coach Ken Hamilton told the press. "I would hate to call anybody better."

Laurinburg coach Frank "Bishop" McDuffie enthused: "He's one of the best, And he's one of the best there's going to be."

Nate McMillan, who later played with Washburn at North Carolina State from 1984 to 1986 and then while with the NBA's Seattle Supersonics, played against Washburn when he was at Laurinburg.

NATE MCMILLAN: "I remember that day like it was yesterday. We were both being recruited by North Carolina State, I was in my sophomore year at Chowan University. NC State set up the game for the two of us to play before an NC State game. Chris was the more recruited guy, so I'm pretty sure the fan base that came to the game came to see Washburn. The building was sold out.

"I probably had one of the best games of my career. We won the game. I can't remember my stats, but I'm sure I had pretty good ones. I never saw Chris play basketball before that game, but I knew he had the reputation as being one of the country's top high school players. Chris was big and could do it all. He could handle the ball. He could run. He was athletic. He could shoot the ball. He could post and had really good footwork in the paint. I hadn't seen anybody like that before… a guy that big who could run the floor as well as he did. He was a player I had never seen the likes of before."

Washburn learned that a scout from the NBA Philadelphia 76ers had attended one of his games. "A guy from the Sixers was here?" Washburn asked a reporter excitedly. "I didn't know that. Some pro teams wrote to me last summer, wishing me good luck as I prepared for college and saying they'd keep an eye on me."

Washburn added, "High school to the pros is a giant step. I'm not ready for that."

Washburn was very willing to show the pro scouts what he offered the NBA. In the spring of 1984, Washburn played in the McDonald's Classic in Los Angeles and Washington DC. Both games are considered pit stops on the highway that showcases the country's high school basketball talent. He also played in the 13th Boston Shootout at Northeastern Mathews Arena in Providence, Rhode Island. A national high school player of the year, Washburn was the center of attention.

Washburn was asked if he was ready?

CHRIS WASHBURN: "I don't see it as being any different. It's been like that since I was 14."

Chris Washburn, one of the country's most recruited high school basketball players had made his choice. With his eye on his dream of playing in the NBA, it would now be up to him to show that playing at North Carolina State was the right choice.

2

UNIVERSITY BOUND

"Imagine you're a kid, not yet out of his teens, and you're getting slipped as much as $4,000 or $5,000 a pop. It was a lot of money, and it was being given to me without my earning it. It was things like that led me to never learning to respect the value of money." ~ Chris Washburn

Chris Washburn was excited about playing for the North Carolina State Wolfpack. He had just garnered his third straight All-American Parade award and had chosen the Wolfpack after being chased by nearly every major university basketball program in the country.

He would follow a long line of noted basketball players to the Athletic Coast Conference (ACC) and NC State, including the Wolfpack's David Thompson, Kenny Carr, and Tom Burleson.

The Wolfpack were still riding high from their momentous 1983 victory. That was two seasons ago, and now, as the team was getting ready for the 1984-85 season, Washburn's freshman year, it was picked to finish fourth in the conference standings. The team knew that it probably had to win the championship in order to make it to the NCAA tournament.

Incredibly, the Wolfpack did just that, as the team battled its way to the championship game against the University of Houston Cougars, nicknamed Phi Slama Jama. It was one of the most exciting games in the NCAA tournament history. The Wolfpack escaped with their second national title after a last-second air ball by Dereck Whittenburg was caught and dunked by Lorenzo Charles. The final score: 54-52.

CHRIS WASHBURN: "The funny thing is I don't watch much basketball on television, but I was caught up in the NCAA tournament when I learned about the Wolf Pack's crazy run. I was excited about the upcoming season knowing that there were still a lot of players from that championship season coming back to play."

Returnees from that 1983 championship season were seniors Lorenzo Charles, Terry Gannon, Cozell McQueen, and juniors Nate McMillan and Ernie Myers.

Myers recalls the excitement surrounding Washburn's coming to North Carolina State:

ERNIE MYERS: "I already had been at State for three years before Chris got there. We had already won a national championship. Chris was a grand prize. I mean, he was one of the top players in the country entering college that year. He was the best center in the country.

"He had signed with us, so we were excited. It was a great time to be playing at NC State. We were winning, although my junior year we didn't make the tournament. So, we were looking forward to Chris coming, and he came along with Nate McMillan and a bunch of other guys, that year.

"It was just an exciting time. We thought we'd win another national championship with Chris in the middle. Yeah, it started off very promising, didn't it? Until Chris started getting in trouble, it looked pretty good."

Washburn had met Jim Valvano, NC State's coach, when Valvano came to Hickory to see him play pickup. Nicknamed Jimmy V, Valvano was one of the rising coaches in college ball. He had been head coach at North Carolina State University for five years and had won that national championship in 1983.

He would be twice voted ACC Coach of the Year and would have a career record of 346 victories and 210 defeats. From 1986 to 1989, he was in charge of sports at N.C. State. However, he lost that position due to a problem involving how athletes were recruited and admitted to the school. After that, he became a sports commentator on TV for ESPN and ABC. Unfortunately, he passed away after fighting cancer for a year.

Valvano and North Carolina State were one of the 150 of the nation's institutions of higher learning who recruited Washburn through visits, phone calls, and a flood of impassioned letters. An article in the *Sports Illustrated* magazine documented the chase for one of the country's most heralded freshmen players.

According to the article, North Carolina State's coach Valvano and his assistant, Tom Abatemarco, bombarded Washburn with 278 letters, urging, almost begging, Washburn to enroll in their school. One of the letters stated that "Valvano 'can be your coach, friend and big brother…. Come and play for a great person and coach." Another letter claimed. "Our winning the national championship has affected the entire country."

Valvano even came to Hickory in person to spin his charm on Washburn.

CHRIS WASHBURN: "It was early summer. Coach V came with his assistant to see me. He had won that national championship in '83 and was in the news a lot, so I knew a lot about him. We talked. I was young, impressionable, but he was the type of guy I could relate to. He was energetic and animated when he talked. He told me I would be a good addition to the team. I would probably start. The team was losing their big man, Thurl Bailey, and all they had was Cozell McQueen. The only other big man they had was John Thompson and he was just 6'9"".

Washburn later visited the NCSU campus while at Laurinburg when the school had played the Wolfpack freshmen team. Washburn was given the royal treatment.

CHRIS WASHBURN: "That was when I met Jim Valvano again. He took me to the gym and played a tape for me of a Wolfpack basketball game. The atmosphere of that game was electric. The crowd was going crazy. Valvano was trying to show me what I could experience if I came to NC State. He didn't have to sell me. I was coming there."

Washburn's mother and his aunt accompanied her son to the university to help settle him in.

CHRIS WASHBURN: "I had been to NC State before, but yeah, it was exciting. The school was still celebrating that 1983 championship, and it was like I was on the team. They showed me the campus and the room I would have. I was going around meeting players from the team. I was making friends. I was just eighteen, but I was being treated as an adult almost."

The university gave Chris his own private room, and he had his own car to drive.

CHUCKY BROWN: "Some of the other players had cars, but we had a lot of juniors and seniors on the team who didn't have their own rooms. Was Chris receiving money on the side? I really don't know. It was something we didn't talk about."

Washburn was indeed receiving money under the table. He was being treated special because of his talent. He did not know who else on the team was getting money, and the players never talked about it.

CHRIS WASHBURN: "I think I got money through the alumni. I would get a thousand dollars every couple of weeks. I never knew where it came from. I got money in tennis shoe boxes. I got money in envelopes. It was never in person. It was illegal, I know. That's why you never mentioned it to anyone because you never knew who you were talking with. Even when I was later suspended, I received money. After my suspension, I never went back to Hickory and stayed on campus because I thought the money would stop coming in."

Washburn believes the money had a negative effect on him.

CHRIS WASHBURN: "Imagine you're a kid, not yet out of his teens, and you're getting slipped as much as $4,000 or $5,000 a pop. It was a lot of money, and it was being given to me without my earning it. It was things like that led me to never learning to respect the value of money."

Washburn did not see anything wrong in taking the money.

CHRIS WASHBURN: "We athletes are workers for the school. We are being exploited. We are bringing in all kinds of money for the school and not getting anything for it. Valvano was getting a check from Nike, and we had to wear the shoe."

Expectations were high for the Wolfpack during Washburn's freshman season. Duke was ranked sixth in the country, and the team was picked by a poll of sports writers and broadcasters to capture the ACC championship. Duke returned the same starting five as of a season ago and added several freshmen who were expected to bolster the bench. North Carolina finished second in the balloting, garnering twenty-five votes for first place.

Valvano was eager to make another bid to the NCAA tournament. His unheralded 1982-83 team had slipped into the postseason and went all the way to the national championship. His 1983-84 team looked like a lock to defend the title with a 19-7 record two weeks into the regular season.

Then disaster struck. The Wolfpack lost its last five regular season games, went out in the first round of the NCAA tournament, and had to settle for the NIT tournament, not the NCAA. To add insult to injury, Florida State came into NC State's Reynolds Coliseum and upset the Wolfpack in the first round.

Given the history, Valvano was cautious about the upcoming season. "I don't think we have a starting team," Valvano said candidly in a press interview. "We have a situational team. Now I have a lot more decisions on the bench."

When asked about Washburn, his prize freshmen recruit, Valvano was candid. "His biggest adjustment is defense, a problem prevalent among freshmen. His offense is so far ahead of his defense that he does things instinctively offensively that defensively need to be taught."

"If Washburn has a fault, it's being too nice," Valvano added. "He's got to get down in the pits and be a blue-collar worker. He's got to get a little more physical. He doesn't want to do that right now, but you don't want to force feed him."

When recruiting Washburn, Valvano had all but assured him that he would be a starter if he came to NC State, but as the season approached, he was not so sure. Valvano told reporters that Washburn would have to fight for time with John Thompson and Lorenzo Charles. So how did Washburn feel about Valvano's comments?

CHRIS WASHBURN: "I wasn't worried about what the coach was saying. Thurl Bailey, one of State's key big men, had just graduated. The only other big man they had besides me was Cozell McQueen. I knew I had a chance to start. I did well in practice and was able to get the starting position. I felt good about myself."

While Washburn was determined to get off to a good start at NC State, he somehow could not stay out of trouble. Problems just started to pop up. He was invited to go to the beach with a good friend. They each brought along a girlfriend with them. They left Raleigh on a Friday and planned to return on a Sunday.

CHRIS WASHBURN: "I had to be back for classes Monday. We were all going to come back by Monday, but they decided to stay a little longer. They persuaded me to stay. I didn't really think about the consequences. I missed some classes and got behind on my schoolwork. It put a lot of pressure on me."

It did not help Washburn that he was a high profile, prominent member of the basketball team and becoming popular at school.

CHRIS WASHBURN: "It was early September. School, let alone basketball season, had not started yet. I began meeting girls, and I was feeling good about myself and maybe a little cocky. I met this young girl. She was older than me, 20 or 21, a junior. I had just turned 18. We kinda hit it off. She took me around the college, and I started to feel comfortable around her, I liked her, but I was hearing that she was seeing other guys. I didn't really like that. I guess I was immature. We started to argue about it. I got angry, lost control, and slapped her. I didn't think it was a hard slap, but she complained to the school. The next thing I knew, I was having to answer to the school administration."

On September 20, 1984, Washburn was convicted of a misdemeanor charge of pushing and slapping the girlfriend. He received a thirty-day suspended sentence and was fined $25 plus court costs.

Coach Valvano decided to assign one of his teammates as a kind of minder who would monitor Washburn's behavior. That job fell to Dereck Whittenburg, one of the heroes of the Wolfpack's 1983 championship win. Whittenburg shot the last-second air ball that was caught and dunked by Lorenzo Charles for the victory. In 1985, Whittenburg would become an assistant coach at NC State under Jim Valvano.

DEREK WHITTENBURG: "I don't know why I was chosen, but coach Valvano asked me if I would look out for Chris. I was to make sure he went to class on time, attend practice, show up for the games. At times it could be irritating, but Wash was a good kid. He accepted it."

CHRIS WASHBURN: "I looked up to Dereck. He was more than a minder or babysitter. He was like the older brother I never had. I valued what he told me."

Still, Washburn could not stay out of trouble. A problem arose when the Wolfpack kicked off its 1984 basketball season by embarking on a series of games against the Greek national team. Four of the games were played in Greece. The Wolfpack left on October 13 for a four-game exhibition tournament, with a three-game tournament in Thessaloniki, Greece. Valvano told the reporter that his team was "going for the enjoyment of the trip, some educational course work and basketball, in that order."

John Riddle, the head of NCSU's University Studies Department would be accompanying the team, and he would conduct special classes and sightseeing tours. The team played four games in Greece, opening the tour in Thessaloniki, Greece, against the Grecian team of PAOK. Washburn played well. In a game against the Greeks in Athens on October 20, Washburn scored 24 points and had eight dunks and ten rebounds in a 90 to 69 exhibition victory.

Washburn's problems with the Greek trip began when team members went into a souvenir store that sold statues, ornaments, and different souvenirs. Washburn thought he would help himself to some of the objects, and he stuffed his pockets before walking out of the store.

CHRIS WASHBURN: "I don't know why I did it. I just liked to make people laugh. My mom would warn me: 'You may think a lot of things you do are funny, but other people won't.' When we were leaving the store, some of my teammates warned me: 'You're gonna get caught.'"

One of those players who warned Washburn was teammate Ernie Myers, who had helped NC State win the national championship in 1983.

ERNIE MYERS: "I saw Chris take the stuff and so I asked him: 'You gonna pay for all that? That guy in the store saw you.' He said: 'Nah, I'm not going to pay.' I told him 'you got to put the stuff back.' Chris just laughed."

CHRIS WASHBURN: "When we got on the bus, one of guys noticed that somebody was following us on a motorbike. It was the store owner. When we got to the hotel, he told one of the coaches what had happened at the store."

Teammate Nate McMillan was on the tour and recalls the incident. The store owner got all of his stuff back. "We went up to our room, and about ten minutes later we got a call. Valvano wanted us downstairs in five minutes. So, we go downstairs and at the meeting the coaches are losing it. Valvano was going crazy, just tearing into us. He said 'I'm leaving the room. I want you guys to find out who stole the stuff and tell me.' The players had a team meeting. Nobody was going to snitch, but eventually Chris admitted to the theft, and the coaches were informed."

CHRIS WASHBURN: "The funny thing was I got no individual punishment. The team got punished. The coach made them run. So, the guys got mad at me. That didn't last long, and they soon got over the incident. But that incident taught me a bad lesson. I thought I could get away with anything and not get into trouble. When I look back on my life, I think it was bad that I was an only child. I mean I had to learn everything on my own. I never had any brothers or sisters teaching or warning me: 'Don't do that. You'll get into trouble.'"

Myers today believes Chris Washburn's life is a sad story, a man with immense talent, a career path that had great promise, but a life and career that would end in great disappointment and tragedy.

ERNIE MYERS: "The kid, if you look at the people around him, he just didn't have any good ones to advise him."

Washburn got off to a solid start on November 24 when the 13th ranked Wolfpack thumped Campbell University 94 to 54. Valvano went to his bench early and often, as the Wolfpack jumped to a 16-6 lead in the first seven minutes and never looked back. The Wolfpack's biggest margin was

88 to 47 when Washburn hit a free throw. The Wolfpack followed up with an easy 93 to 70 victory over Santa Barbara. Washburn led his team with 16 points.

The Wolfpack won six of its first seven games, losing only to Georgia Tech in a thriller, 66 to 64. In the first seven games, Washburn averaged 10.7 points and 5. 9 rebounds. On December 11, Washburn was selected ACC Rookie of the Week in wins over North Carolina A&T and Western Carolina. He hit 12 out of 25 shots with six free throws.

CHRIS WASHBURN: "I was confident, arrogant, in fact, about my ability to play. For being rookie of the week, I got a plague and some attention. I knew I could play the game. So winning rookie of the week was no surprise to me."

Washburn was averaging over six rebounds a game in just 22.3 minutes of playing time. Washburn's solid play was enough to convince Valvano to keep the freshman in the starting lineup.

The team was expecting big things from the young basketball prodigy. He was lucky to escape serious punishment for the girlfriend slapping incident and for the Greek theft incident. But then in December 1984, his lucky streak ended. Washburn became involved in an embarrassing incident that would derail his career.

On December 21, 1984, Chris Washburn was arrested on charges of breaking into an athletic dormitory room and stealing five pieces of stereo equipment that was later determined to be worth $800.

CHRIS WASHBURN: "The room was occupied by William West and Jeffrey Davis, football players at NC State. I knew they had a stereo in their room. I thought it would be a good joke if I took the stereo. I wasn't planning on keeping it. So, I snuck through his window, grabbed the stereo, put it outside the window and jumped out. I then took the stereo and left.

"I was planning to put the stereo back eventually. I thought that would end the matter. Well, the roommate came back to the room and saw that the stereo was missing. But instead of calling the campus police, he called the city police, and it became a big incident. I was nervous because I had been in trouble before when I slapped that girlfriend. When I got to my apartment with the stereo, the police were waiting for me. I was arrested and taken to jail."

It was the real world for Chris Washburn. Jim Valvano could not protect him. Washburn was interrogated by the police, just as any other suspect accused of theft would be. In a twenty-seven-minute taped interrogation, Washburn told the police, "I was going to give it back." Washburn's defense contended it was a stupid prank, and that Washburn should be left off lightly. But Washburn ended up spending time in jail.

CHRIS WASHBURN: "It was awful. I had to spend about a day and a half in jail. I was in the cell by myself. No contact with anybody. I had time to think. If I had any sense, it should have been a time for me to reflect on how I got to that jail cell. But it would take me a long time before I would do any reflection on my life. The sad part: My life would eventually get worse."

Washburn was charged with second-degree burglary. The judge gave him a suspended six-year sentence and placed him on probation for five years. Meanwhile, Washburn would remain in school and on scholarship.

The trial took place on February 4, 1985. At trial, Washburn's defense attorney, Wade Smith, told the judge that "this young man has to be punished. He recognizes that. While there must be punishment, we hope the punishment does not close the doors to his future."

Washburn faced a maximum sentence of forty years in prison, but he was sentenced to a mere forty-six hours in jail after he pleaded guilty to three misdemeanor charges stemming from the theft of the stereo equipment. The judge also sentenced Washburn to a jail term that coincided with the anniversary of the incident. The term would begin at 6 pm, Thursday, December 19, and end on December 21 at 4 pm. That was the time during which the stereo was reported missing.

Under the terms of his probation, Washburn had to perform 200 hours of community service at a center for retarded children in Raleigh and twenty hours washing and refueling police squad cars. The sentence also included provisions that he get mental health treatment and pay $1,000 to a crime victim's fund.

The judge asked Savannah, Washburn's mother, who sat behind him in court if he was guilty of the charges, and she responded, "Yes, sir."

NC State struggled with what to do with Chris Washburn. The university was mum, and Valvano refused to comment on the situation. On his weekly radio show, Valvano told the press: "I, myself, have no comment at this time. It's a university matter right now. It would be inappropriate for me for me to make any comments at this time. When the timing is appropriate, we will certainly do so. Maybe next week, but not tonight."

The university left Washburn's possible return to the team up to Valvano. The coach said he would ask professional counselors to recommend what would be in Washburn's best interest. "Some professional opinions, I believe, are important," Valvano said. He did not give a timetable for his decision.

On February 8, Valvano got into a confrontation with a two-man television crew outside his office. Valvano grabbed the camera lens and berated the reporter. The footage was aired on television that night. Valvano defended his action, claiming the reporters were hounding Washburn and that they were "very rude."

Meanwhile, the controversy widened to include the North Carolina State's admissions standards for athletes when Washburn's academic records were entered into the public court records. The records showed that Washburn's combined SAT score was 470, which placed him in the lower five percent of males in the nation who took the test. The score, 470, was well below the 1,030 average achieved by freshmen entering the university. His high school grades consisted mostly of D's and F's in the ninth, tenth, and 11th grades, improving to Bs and Cs in 12th grade after transferring to Laurinburg Institute. Washburn's IQ was listed as eighty-six, based on a test Washburn had taken in the sixth grade. The records also showed that Washburn had a learning disability in the "language area."

All of the revelations about his academic record were embarrassing to Washburn, but he refused to let it phase him.

CHRIS WASHBURN: "I had an aunt who would tell me 'no matter what you do in life, keep your head up. You're too big to walk slumped over and your head down. So, whatever you do in life, keep your head up and shoulders back.' So, whatever was said about me, especially in the media, I always did that."

On February 21, North Carolina State announced that Chris Washburn would not return to the team in 1985. In a news release Valvano said, "After consulting with the many professional people involved, I have concluded that Chris must concentrate on his community service obligations and on his academic work."

Valvano told reporters that Washburn would be expected to return to the team next season. "The university and our basketball program will continue to support Chris Washburn in any and every way that we feel will be beneficial to his future."

A couple of days later, state officials announced that they may launch an investigation into the practice of admitting athletes with embarrassing low grades into state colleges. Two members of the North Carolina General Assembly wanted students to score at least 700 on the Scholastic Aptitude Test before they were admitted to any university in the North Carolina system.

"Anyone who cannot obtain a 700 on the SAT does not belong in a university," Representative Frank Rhodes told the press. "They should be in a vocational school."

Representative John Church, chairperson of the House Higher Education Committee, said, "We ought not kill the possibility of someone becoming a great basketball player because he's having difficulties with his studies. We can offer him tutoring, five years instead of four years of study and that goes for any group of students."

University of North Carolina President Joe Friday revealed that he had been trying for several years to convince the NCAA to rule all athletes who do not score at least 700 on the Scholastic Aptitude Test ineligible to play ball their first year of school.

The Washburn case caused controversy in North Carolina as people debated Washburn's treatment by the courts and whether he should be allowed to play for the Wolfpack.

Some felt that Washburn was being treated as a special individual instead of an ordinary citizen. Regardless of who he is, some citizens felt he did the wrong thing and should not have the special privileges he had before. The three-day jail sentence and community service work are not enough punishment, they believed, to justify what he did.

Supporters of Washburn, on the other hand, argued that stealing a stereo was not as bad a crime as, say, rape or murder. They also complained about the release of Washburn's SAT scores. Hardy D. Barry, the assistant vice chancellor at North Carolina State, acknowledged in a press interview that "some teachers at North Carolina State had misgivings about how the Washburn affair was handled and that Washburn had been 'unduly punished.' His privacy had been invaded. He's been made to seem like he is some kind of pariah. And, in fact, he's a conventional athlete."

In an interview with the *Raleigh News and Observer* newspaper, Valvano admitted that the incident was hurting his team. "The aura or atmosphere of what's happening to Chris…detracts from what we're trying to accomplish," Valvano explained.

Slowly, the furor and attention over Washburn and his grades and the stolen stereo subsided as North Carolina State focused on the rest of the 1984-85 season.

The 1985 NCAA Division I men's basketball tournament involved sixty-four schools playing in single-elimination play to determine the national champion of the men's NCAA Division I college basketball. It was the first year the field was expanded to 64 teams, from 53 in the previous year's tournament. It began on March 15.

The Wolfpack were the third seed in the West. They beat Nevada in the first round 65-56. The Wolfpack continued their winning ways beating UTEP in the second round and reaching the regional semifinal by defeating the University of Alabama.

Without their star freshman, the Wolfpack had reached the Final Eight. Could another miracle run like the fabled 1983 Wolfpack team be in the works? It was not meant to be, as the Wolfpack lost the west regional final 69-60 to #1 seed St. John's University. Villanova defeated Georgetown by a score of 66–64 to win their first-ever national championship, in what is considered by analysts to be one of the biggest upsets in tournament history.

The Wolfpack had experienced an outstanding season and post-season tournament. But for the team, it had also been a frustrating experience.

ERNIE MYERS: "Our (1984-85) team was a good one. But if we could have had Chris Washburn playing the season would have been outstanding and given us a shot at the national championship."

With his suspension, Washburn sat out the year on the Wolfpack bench and had a chance to observe the 1985 season up close. It was frustrating to him as well.

CHRIS WASHBURN: "I knew I could get out there and play. I knew I could help. So, you know it was frustrating every time we lost. I knew that if we lost anywhere between ten or fifteen points, I could have made those points up if I was playing. When I went into next year, I had a chip on my shoulder. I had something to prove."

3

RETURN TO ACTION

"Everybody was excited about the future and were looking to next year because we had a lot of guys coming back, and we had some good talent coming in." ~ Chris Washburn

By the summer of 1985, Chris Washburn had completed his community service punishment and was enrolled in summer school. He had kept busy and stayed out of trouble.

CHRIS WASHBURN: "I stayed on campus during the suspension. Most of the students probably thought I was in school. They would see me around at the student center or walking around campus. They knew who I was. I didn't feel out of place. I was still practicing, playing basketball. I was raring to go. I thought I had something to prove to the team, to coach Valvano, to the ACC and to the NCAA. I had a chip on my shoulder because, you know, at that time, I'd already heard all the things that I was supposed to be, how I was a special ed student, a kind of dummy, and all that kind of stuff. I knew what they were saying about me and my SAT scores."

Washburn worked a construction job and paid half his earnings to the court. He did 420 hours of community service work, including work with mentally retarded children. In an interview with the *Charlotte Observer,* Washburn recalled, "Once I went out on the court, and we got into the flow of the game, and after I got a couple baskets or a few rebounds, my nerves kinda calmed down."

CHRIS WASHBURN: "I was feeling really good about myself. I thought things were going to work out for me. What I had done was in the past. Now I could look back and see the mistakes I've made. I'm used to the pressure. It made me wise up, mature a lot faster. And I'm glad it happened at an early age. I had another chance to play."

In early October, Washburn was quietly reinstated by the Wolfpack team. He had completed his court-ordered community service, as well as other requirements of his sentence, and had made sufficient academic progress to return to the team.

Valvano told the press, "He's a regularly enrolled student at North Carolina State with all of the privileges that go with it. As far as basketball goes, at this point, he has fulfilled all the obligations imposed by the state, by the university, and by our ball club, and he is welcome to come out October 15."

Washburn had not exactly fulfilled all his obligations relating to the stereo incident. He was convicted of larceny and still had to serve a jail term from 6 p.m., December 19, to 4 p.m., December 21. The dates were chosen as a one-year anniversary for the 1984 stereo theft incident. North Carolina State was concerned that the jail term conflicted with a scheduled game that the Wolfpack had with Wake Forest on December 19. The court indicated it had no objection to changing Washburn's jail time.

With Chris Washburn back in the lineup, the Wolfpack were highly optimistic about the upcoming season, even though there would be just two seniors on the team. Gone were the team's top three scorers and two leading rebounders, but Valvano had recruited an outstanding freshmen class, and he loved their attitude. "The last two years we had a lot of talent, but you wouldn't see me bring a tuba or brass band to practice," Valvano told the press. "It was more like going to the dentist. I enjoy kids who joke and laugh and enjoy the game."

Valvano said the team was the best he has had since coming to North Carolina State. He predicted that by the end of the year, the team would be "pretty good."

Valvano had just had an inter-team scrimmage when he made those remarks. Chris Washburn had led the Red Squad over the White Squad with 27 points and 14 rebounds in a dominating display. Washburn looked like the dominating big man he was predicted to be when he first came to NC State.

Ranked 17th in the AP poll, the Wolfpack opened the season with an easy victory over Western Carolina, 80-57. The team was led by one of the two returning seniors, Nate McMillan, with 19 points on 9-11 shooting from the floor and six rebounds. Washburn played 33 minutes and finished with 13 points and four rebounds. There was some drama when Washburn and Western Carolina center Andre Gault got tangled.

CHRIS WASHBURN: "I felt no pressure coming back, except for the pressure that I put on myself. It was a non-conference game, but the nerves were still there. I was nervous about playing in front of 14,000 fans. I'm expecting myself to play well, but this is my first game back. Once I got a couple baskets and a dunk, and I got into the flow of the game, I kind of settled in. I told myself: I can do this."

North Carolina State followed up that opening game with an impressive 94-56 victory over Furman University. Washburn led the Wolfpack, now ranked 14th, with 20 points. He also had eight rebounds and three blocked shots.

The schedule got tougher on December 2 when the Wolfpack beat Tampa, but they lost to Loyola and Florida State on November 30 and December 4, bringing their record to 3-2. On December 7, the Wolfpack faced powerful number seven, the University of Kansas, in Greensboro, North Carolina. The Wolfpack lost 76-67, but it was not because of the play of Chris Washburn, which drew rave reviews. The true freshman scored 22 points.

One college coach noted after the game, "Washburn is playing like a man who knows what probation means. He realizes he's been given his last chance. His play, his work ethic, his attitude is extraordinary."

North Carolina State chose to play in the Chaminade Classic during the holidays. In an upset, the Wolfpack beat 12th ranked Nevada-Las Vegas 80-73 for the championship. The game, however, proved to be too much for the Wolfpack. Nate McMillan twisted his ankle. Ernie Myers had stomach cramps and a shoulder injury, and Bennie Bolton had second-half fall trouble.

Then there was the case of coach Valvano. He fainted toward the end of the game when he jumped up to give instructions. Valvano joked that he took the mandatory eight count. Washburn again starred, scoring 17 points, snaring 13 rebounds, and receiving the most valuable player award.

Washburn's play continued to draw accolades in the press, even though he had made it a policy not to speak to the media. Speculation arose about whether Washburn would be turning pro after the season. People waited eagerly in anticipation of Washburn matchups with University of North Carolina's Brad Daugherty and Georgia Tech's John Salley, debating how his performances would affect his NBA draft eligibility.

For Washburn, speculation about him turning pro was idle talk.

CHRIS WASHBURN: "Honestly, at the time, I never really thought about turning pro. I really expected to return to NC State for my third year."

On December 28, a day after the team returned from the Chaminade tournament in Hawaii, Washburn began spending time in the Wake County jail as part of the sentence he received for stealing the stereo. Washburn's mother, Savannah, and the North Carolina State basketball team had successfully petitioned Wake County Judge J. Milton Read to postpone the jail term so that Washburn could play in a nationally televised game against Wake Forest. Washburn was released on December 29.

The following day, the Wolfpack crushed Monmouth University 106-63 at State's Reynold Coliseum, finishing as they entered the new year with an eight and three record. The Wolfpack led by as much as twenty-four points while playing its entire roster in the first twenty minutes. Washburn had thirteen points. North Carolina State had now won five games after a three-and-three start, upsetting the nationally ranked University of Nevada, Las Vegas. Washburn finished the first eleven games with an impressive 17.6 scoring average.

The new year for the Wolfpack would start out by playing the powerful University of North Carolina Tar Heels, ranked number one in the country. The Tar Heels were led by seven-foot Brad Daugherty, a star center projected to be the top draft pick in the 1986 NBA draft. Nicknamed "The Big Train," Daughtery would be one of the greatest big men ever to play for the University of North Carolina.

The game marked North Carolina's final home game in the 10,000-seat Carmichael Auditorium. The Tar Heels would move from the auditorium to their new 21,000-seat Student Activities Center with a game on January 18 against number three Duke, North Carolina, 14-0 overall and 1-0 in the ACC, failed to be distracted by pre-game publicity and proceeded to tear into North Carolina State.

The Wolfpack led 19-9 midway through the first half before the Tar Heels reeled off 10 straight points. North Carolina's Joe Wolf's baseline jumper 9:55 into the game tied the score 19-19. Leading 39-36 at halftime, North Carolina broke the game open with a 7-0 spurt over a three-minute span in the second half. A jump shot from the key by forward Joe Wolf put the Tar Heels ahead 80-69 with 3:10 to play. North Carolina State never got closer than nine points after that.

Brad Daugherty scored a game-high 28 points, while Chris Washburn led NC State with 21 points. Neither player had trouble scoring on the other. After the game, the two giant centers had complimentary things to say about each other.

"I know Chris, and I like him, but I had never played against him," said Daugherty, "He's good. I heard that he was a forward trapped in a center's body. I guess he is. I didn't know he could shoot like that."

Daugherty, the senior against whom Washburn would be measured, did say that Washburn could improve his shot selection a bit. Washburn, in turn, said Daugherty was the best center he had ever played against.

The Wolfpack's next game against North Carolina A&T was supposed to be a nice breather before they began play in the tough ACC conference. The Wolfpack were to play the undefeated and third-ranked Duke Blue Devils in two days. The game saw a subpar performance by Chris Washburn, who managed just six points.

CHRIS WASHBURN: "We were coming off a really big game and thinking about a big one on Saturday. We knew we weren't playing up to our potential, but it was kind of hard to get up our intensity. We knew we couldn't let this happen again or we might get upset."

Disappointed in their win against North Carolina A&T, the Wolfpack rolled into Cameron Indoor Stadium to take on the Blue Devils. Washburn knew he would face a hostile crowd that was more than willing to shower abuse on him.

Bob Lipper, a writer with the *Richmond Times Dispatch*, described the atmosphere at Cameron Indoor Stadium graphically: "Populated by several thousand maniacs who masquerade weekdays as Duke students, it is the home of fear and loathing in the ACC. No visiting player with a rap sheet or complex problems or a weak constitution is safe."

Washburn tried to get mentally ready for the game.

CHRIS WASHBURN: "Most of the players told me to expect anything. I was more or less anxious to see what they (the Duke fans) were going to do, but it really wasn't that bad. I didn't pay any attention. I just tried to play hard."

Sure enough, Washburn was taunted, booed mercilessly, and even pelted with ice as he left the floor. The Blue Devil mascot wheeled a shopping cart onto the floor advertised as the "N.C. State Mobile Stereo Warehouse." And when Washburn was whistled for a foul, students shouted "guilty, guilty."

CHRIS WASHBURN: "We are sitting on the bench waiting for the game to start, and the lights go out. It was pitch dark, and I felt a knot in my stomach. One of our players sitting next to me, nudges me and said 'Oh, oh.' Then a spotlight comes on. A guy comes bouncing out of the door in a convict outfit. And he was pulling a wagon behind him filled with a stereo and records. He pulled it across court, and the crowd applauded enthusiastically. It didn't upset me, but it got me ready to play the game. I knew I had to silence the crowd. A couple of dunks would do it."

But Washburn was guarded closely, and he took only seven shots. Three of them came during the second half, and they were separated by a fourteen-minute stretch when he was stopped cold without an attempt. Washburn also committed five turnovers.

Senior forward Mark Alarie led all Duke players with 24 points, and All-American guard Johnny Dawkins added 17 to pace third-ranked and undefeated Duke past NC State 74-64.

Wolfpack was ahead 18-15 midway through the first half, but Duke went on a 10-1 run to take the lead for good. Duke's record improved to 14-0 overall—its best start ever—and 3-0 in the Atlantic Coast Conference.

Forward Ernie Myers scored 16 points and grabbed a game-high nine rebounds to lead the Wolfpack, now 9 -5 overall and 1-2 in the ACC. Senior guard Nate McMillan scored 12 points for NC State, while center Chris Washburn and forward Teviin Binns each added 11 points.

The Wolfpack returned to its winning ways four days later with a close-fought 60 to 57 victory over Clemson; after Clemson had opened a 18-10 lead, Washburn took a single shot, a jump-hook from the right base line that hit the side of the backboard.

Valvano called time out. The Wolfpack went to Washburn the next two possessions, and he missed a shot while converting a foul into two made free throws. Shortly after that, Valvano benched Washburn for the final 10 minutes of the period.

Clemson's sagging defense yielded no field goals to Washburn, who had four points. Washburn was in a slump. In the two games before Clemson, Washburn had just nine field-goal attempts and scored a total of 17 points.

The Wolfpack had a scare when Washburn fell to the floor on the last play of the game and bruised his knee. He was expected to play the next game against Wake Forest.

The Wolfpack were now in the brutal part of the ACC schedule. No team would be easy to play. On January 18, N.C. State hung on to beat the Wake Forest Deacons 45-44.

Wolfpack guard Bennie Bolton missed the first half of a one-and-one with five seconds remaining to give the Deacons a final chance. But Wake Forest did not have a final time-out, and Mark Cline's long jump shot, which hit the back of the rim, was launched a millisecond after the buzzer.

On January 23, the Wolfpack faced the University of Maryland at the Cole Field House in College Park, Maryland. The game would pit Washburn against Maryland's superstar Len Bias. Driesell's team had opened the Atlantic Coast Conference season with a school-record six losses. The Terrapins finally won their first conference game on January 28 when they beat hapless Wake Forest by twenty-two points at home.

Washburn had heard of Len Bias but had never met him. Washburn decided to walk around campus and look for him.

CHRIS WASHBURN: "Len had a reputation that was almost bigger than life. He was getting out of class, and we met. We chatted a bit and said we'd see each other on the court. I was surprised that he didn't look that big. But then I got on the court with him, and I saw how cut and chilled he was. He didn't play particularly well that game, but I was impressed with him."

Bias had arrived at the University of Maryland raw and undisciplined but with a world of potential. He was considered a dynamic player, a guaranteed lock as an early first-round pick in the NBA draft, if not the first pick. But Bias would lead a secret life that ultimately later led to tragedy. It would ensnare Washburn.

Early in the 1985-86 season, Len Bias had been the Terps' only consistent player, leading the league in scoring with an average of 22.3 points. He played the entire game against the Wolfpack but had to work hard to score 16 points, hitting on only six of fifteen shots. Washburn added 16 points for the Wolfpack.

The Wolfpack lost 67-55, but the score was tight for most of the game. With the game tied 45-45 with 9:22 left, the Terps had an 11-2 surge that put the team in front to stay. The Pack failed to score during a 4:08 stretch late in the game, with a Len Bias basket breaking that drought with 4:15 remaining. The Pack did not score again until fifty-eight seconds were left, and the Terps were out of reach.

The Terps scored eight straight points late in the first half for a 28-19 advantage and held a 35-31 halftime lead. The Wolfpack record was 12-5 overall and 4-2 in the ACC.

Coach Valvano was pleased with his Wolfpack's performance. After the game, he explained, "I thought it was critical for us to stay in our game plan. Sometimes a young team has trouble doing that. Our plan was to change defenses often, stay on Lenny Bias all night and not let him take control down the stretch. Offensively, we wanted to get the ball inside."

Two days after their Terrapins triumph, the Wolfpack returned home to beat the University of Virginia Cavaliers. Chris Washburn scored 15 points, and North Carolina State held Virginia to four points over the final six minutes to spearhead a 55-53 Atlantic Coast Conference victory.

Washburn played against another star player, Olden Polynice.

CHRIS WASHBURN: "Polynice was a damn good player. He was difficult to guard."

For the next game, the Wolfpack entertained the talented number 3 Georgia Tech Yellow Jackets, which was enjoying a good season. Georgia Tech was cold as the game began, missing three of their first five shots and turning the ball over three times in the first five minutes.

Georgia Tech, however, eased away to a 44-34 lead with 13:35 to play. NC State made a brief run to cut it to six, but the Yellow Jackets quickly built the lead again, and the Wolfpack could get no closer than nine points in the last four minutes. The final score: Georgia Tech 67, North Carolina State 54.

Several observers noted the great play of Washburn. Bobby Cremins, Georgia Tech coach, simply enthused, "He's a great player."

Georgia Tech star John Salley was impressed playing against Washburn. "Washburn's as good as I thought he would be," Salley told one reporter.

After his college career, Salley made history in the NBA by being the first player to win championships with three different teams. He also uniquely won those championships across three different decades.

Washburn was being credited with much of the Wolfpack success. At this stage of the season, he was leading the team in scoring (15.5), rebounding (7.2) and field-goal percentage (55.9).

Valvano described Washburn as a very coachable and likable kid but noted that he had exercised poor judgment in the past and did not appreciate the public nature of an athlete's life off the court.

NATE MCMILLAN: "I really don't think Chris understood that when you're playing Division I basketball for an institution like N. C. State, people are watching everything you do. You've got to carry yourself in a nice fashion whether you're in uniform or not."

Washburn had decided that he would not talk about basketball with the press. He would simply turn and walk away when asked about his past troubles.

There was no let-up in the Wolfpack schedule as they next faced the number 3 University of Kentucky Wildcats, which was playing their third opponent in five days.

Wolfpack won another close game, 54-51. Kentucky was led by star Kenneth Walker, who had a 19.8 scoring average. Nicknamed "Sky" Walker, he was a first-team consensus All-American as a senior in 1986, and twice he was named the player of the year in the Southeastern Conference. He was selected by the Knicks in the first round of the 1986 NBA draft with the fifth overall pick. North Carolina State beat eighth-ranked Kentucky 54-51 for its second Top 20 upset. Washburn, meanwhile, scored 16 points and played a solid game.

The Wolfpack now headed into a challenging few weeks of play. They were ranked 19th in the country and fourth in the ACC at 5-3 and 14-6 overall. After playing Clemson, they would have to deal with Virginia, Georgia Tech, and Oklahoma, with all of the games on the road.

At Clemson, N.C. State staggered through the final minute of regulation, then got back on its feet in overtime for a 73-69 ACC college basketball victory. The Wolfpack had blown a six-point lead in the final minute of regulation. Bennie Bolton scored six of his seventeen points in overtime, and Charles Shackleford added five of his thirteen in the extra period. Chris Washburn added a respectable eighteen points to help the Wolfpack rally for the win.

Speculation was beginning to heat up about the upcoming NCAA basketball tournament. Basketball observers predicted that the Big Ten would lead with six bids, while the ACC probably would get five: North Carolina, Georgia Tech, Duke, Virginia, and N.C. State, with Clemson and Maryland holding outside chances if they had strong finishes. The Big East and Southeastern Conference also figured to have five teams selected.

The Wolfpack were now unranked and trying hard to earn recognition worthy of being one of the sixty-four teams playing in the NCAA tournament. Louisville, led by fifteen-year veteran coach Denny Crum, also is 15-6 after a 103-68 trouncing of No. 15 Virginia Tech in a Metro Conference battle. Senior Milt Wagner leads the Louisville attack, averaging 15.4 points per game. Billy Thompson, booed at a recent home game for less than sparkling play, was the second-leading scorer at 13.9.

Washburn scored a career-high twenty-seven points as NC State knocked off 16th-ranked Louisville 76-64. Washburn hit ten of fourteen field-goal attempts, exploiting Cardinal freshman Pervis Ellison and almost anyone else from Louisville who came near him. On defense, he flashed quickness and aggressiveness and even came up with four steals, including a deflection of a pass near midcourt, which he followed with a breakaway dunk.

CHRIS WASHBURN: "I was really shocked with their play. On film, they looked a lot tougher."

Now 16-6, the Wolfpack looked headed for the top twenty polls. They had captured seven of its last eight outings.

NC State Wolfpack headed into a challenging few weeks of play. They were now ranked 19th in the country and fourth in the ACC at 5-3 and 14-6 overall. They were headed to Clemson and then would have to deal with Virginia, Georgia Tech, and Oklahoma on the road.

At Clemson, N.C. State staggered through the final minute of regulation, then got back on its feet in overtime for a 73-69 ACC college basketball victory. The Wolfpack blew a six-point lead in the final minute of regulation.

Bennie Bolton scored six of his seventeen points in overtime, and Charles Shackleford added five of his thirteen in the extra period. Chris Washburn added a respectable 18 points.

Speculation was humming about the upcoming NCAA Basketball tournament. Maryland held an outside chance of making the tournament, but it would have to have a strong finish to succeed. Their prospect did not look good as they came to Raleigh and Reynolds Coliseum to face the 17th ranked Wolfpack. Bias carried the Terrapins to a 65-64 lead, then hit a pair of free throws with 1:26 remaining, that gave Maryland the final margin of victory.

"It feels good to win one," Bias said after the game. "It feels like we won the national championship." Maryland would make the NCAA tournament, losing in the second round to the University of Nevada, Las Vegas 70-64.

There was no time for the Wolfpack to rest. Two days later, the team was back at Reynolds Coliseum, hosting the powerful number two Duke Blue Devils, which was carrying a seven-game winning streak into the game. The Wolfpack was expected to rely heavily on Chris Washburn, as they had done in recent weeks. Washburn was leading his team in scoring with 15.4 points a game, rebounding with 7.2 per game, and had 55.0 percent in field goal accuracy.

Robert Sorrels, a counselor associated with the Wake County Justice system, attested to the progress that Washburn had made since the stereo-stealing incident. Sorrels had worked with Washburn. "It's been a year on February 4 that he's been sentenced, and it's been a very satisfying year as far as I'm concerned," Sorrels told the *Greenville News*. "Chris has done a lot of work and weathered a lot of adversity. He's put this behind him. He takes things in stride more."

Dereck Whittenburg, whom Valvano assigned to be Washburn's minder during the '84-85 season thought Washburn had changed as well.

DERECK WHITTENBURG: "I think he did try to change his attitude and his life. It's called becoming mature. Chris realized he had to abide by some rules.

Sometimes when you get in trouble, it puts your career on the line. You're close to being incarcerated, and that will change you. It will straighten you out pretty quick. So, yeah, I think he matured some and that helped him get through that year (the 1985-1986 season). It looked like Chris would go on to be one of NC State's greatest players, talent wise, maybe at least second or third behind David Thompson, number one and Kenny Carr, number two."

Washburn and NC State came up short as they lost a thriller to the Blue Devils 72-70. Duke's Johnny Dawkins hit two free throws with two seconds left to nail the victory. Washburn missed a short jumper from the left of the lane with about thirty-five seconds left. Since the game was played in Raleigh, Washburn did not face any of the harassment he faced earlier at Duke.

The Wolfpack must have been looking ahead to its big showdown with the University of North Carolina Tar Heels on February 23, for the team was stunned in its next outing on February 19 against the University of Virginia, losing 69-60. The Cavaliers broke away from NC State with a 10-2 run in the final three minutes. Washburn had done his part, hitting nine of fifteen shots for eighteen points to go along with six rebounds and three steals.

Valvano was philosophical about the loss, telling the press, "It was a heck of a game until the last three minutes. At that point they did some really good things, and we did not."

The Wolfpack, now out of the rankings, had no time to dwell on the disappointing loss. The big showdown with the University of North Carolina was next on its agenda. The Wolfpack had lost three games in a row, but once again, the team and their star, Chris Washburn, would be facing the number one Tar Heels and their superstar, Brad Daugherty.

The game was special. It was the seniors' last home game. The game was also dedicated to Willis Casey, whom Valvano would be replacing as North Carolina State athletic director. Valvano downplayed the significance of the game. He thought the Wolfpack had done enough to get into the NC tournament.

Chris Washburn did not disappoint with his performance. He dominated the show with 26 points as the Wolfpack beat the Tar Heels 76-65. At one point, the Wolfpack held a 48-

31 lead with 15:05 left to play. Daugherty scored twenty-three points but was outplayed by Washburn.

Valvano was lavish in his praise of Washburn. "Wash had a heck of a game," he enthused. "I think this is the best basketball game he's played."

Washburn agreed with Valvano's assessment.

CHRIS WASHBURN: "Yeah, I think it was my best game. I was really focused. I was just now starting to understand college basketball. It took a little time for me to do that. I was starting to do more positive things. I was in the weight room, for example. I started to take on a leadership role."

The Wolfpack closed the season with two losses, losing to number four Georgia Tech 69-57 on February 27 and to number fourteen University of Oklahoma 72-69, a game in which Washburn led all scorers with twenty points.

Though not on the fence to make the NCAA tournament, the Wolfpack could enhance their position with victories. Georgia Tech was ranked by the Associated Press in a third-place tie with the University of North Carolina.

Four days later, the Wolfpack were in Norman, Oklahoma, where they closed out the regular season with a close 72-69 loss to the 14th ranked University of Oklahoma Sooners. It was heartbreaking loss as a basket by Tim McCalister—his only basket in seven second-half tries—with thirty-four seconds sealed the victory. Washburn led all scorers with twenty-two points and seven rebounds.

The Wolfpack waited to see if they would get a bid to the NCAA Tournament, not totally sure they were in. They had lost six of their last seven games. Their only victory was an important one against the then number-one ranked University of North Carolina Tar Heels. Their won-loss record was 18-12, and they held victories over number eight Kentucky, number sixteen Louisville, and number one University of North Carolina. Would it be enough to push them into the tournament?

Meanwhile, in early March, awards were announced. Washburn was named to the second-team All-ACC, and a little while later, the UPI selected Washburn an honorable mention All-American.

When the final selections for the tournament were made, Duke was given a number one seed and chosen as one of the favorites to reach the Final Four. The Wolfpack was predicted to be a dark horse and given little chance to advance. Washburn was selected as one of the players who would go through hardship after the tournament, even after he had publicly said that he had every intention of returning to NC State.

CHRIS WASHBURN: "As I said, I was really focused on playing. I really had not thought about the offseason. I wasn't nervous because, again, it's just basketball. I felt good."

The 1986 NCAA tournament began on March 13, 1986, and ended with the championship game on March 31 in Dallas, Texas. The 1986 NCAA tournament was the second NCAA tournament with a sixty-four-team bracket, after the NCAA tournament expanded from fifty-three teams in 1984 to 64 teams in 1985.

That tournament was the first time they used a timer to force teams to shoot the ball faster. Before that, teams could hold onto the ball as long as they wanted. In 1986, they started with a 45-second timer. Then, in 1994, they made it even faster, changing the timer to 35 seconds.

The University of North Carolina was seeded six in the Midwest Regional. It would compete against powerhouses the University of Kansas (number one) with All American superstar Danny Manning, the University of Michigan (number 2) with Roy Tarpley and Glen Rice, and Georgetown University Hoyas (number 3) with its well-balanced lineup.

The Wolfpack took on Iowa State in Minneapolis, Minnesota, in the first round. Iowa coach George Raveling downplayed the impact of Chris Washburn, claiming there were other players as good, if not better than him, in the tournament. Washburn responded by scoring eighteen points and igniting a 10-0 spurt midway through the second half that gave the Wolfpack the lead for good on their way to a 66-64 victory. In all, Washburn had twenty-two points.

"I just felt good all night," Washburn said, exhibiting the confidence he had gained during the year. "They left me on the foul line for a while. Then, when they came to me, I could dribble around them and pull up for a short jumper or take it to the hole. I don't believe anybody can stop me one on one."

Two days later, the Wolfpack played their second-round game, toughing it out in a 66-64 victory over the fourteen-ranked University of Arkansas at Little Rock. The Wolfpack was led by Benny Bolton, who scored twenty-three of his twenty-four points after halftime, including twelve in two overtime periods. Washburn supported Bolton with twenty-two points.

In the end, it was the Wolfpack's height and depth that made the difference, as they wore down their opponent. Still, Valvano felt lucky to win.

The Wolfpack were on their way to Kansas City and the Sweet 16. They joined with Duke from the ACC. North

Carolina, Maryland, Virginia, and Georgia Tech had all been eliminated.

On March 21, the Wolfpack faced number seven Iowa State. It was the Wolfpacks' inside game versus Iowa States' running game. Iowa State running game did not work, and the Wolfpacks inside game did. Iowa State had one player over 6' 5". The Wolfpack pounded their way to a 70-66 victory. Washburn put in eighteen points.

Manning was a great player for Kansas, but after that game, Washburn felt he could play against anybody.

CHRIS WASHBURN: "The biggest person I had played to date was Greg Dreiling for Kansas. He was about 7'1" and I even blocked one of his shots. I thought, you know, I can play this game. But, again, we still lost to them. I wasn't into the ego game. My happiness came when the whole team won."

The Wolfpack were now going to the Elite 8 in Kansas City, where they would be facing number 2 University of Kansas in what would virtually be their home court.

Washburn was familiar with Kansas star Danny Manning.

CHRIS WASHBURN: "I got to know Danny from the McDonald's All-American game where we played together. We went to the same Five-Star basketball camps. I always thought Danny had a good college game. He would also have a good NBA game. Danny was a little different than me. I'm more outgoing, more talkative. I like to laugh. He was a little more reserved, a little quieter, but then again, I can't really assess him because I wasn't really in Danny's circle."

Kansas took the game 75-67, with Valvano blaming the loss on defensive breakdowns, possibly fatigue-related. As Nate

McMillan explained, "We played them just right until the last eight minutes. Then we got slack in our defense."

Washburn thought the Wolfpack should have won the game.

CHRIS WASHBURN: "We were winning the game all the way up to maybe the last three or four minutes, but then I stopped getting the ball. They couldn't get the ball to me. That's how Kansas came back."

The Wolfpack took the loss hard, but the team felt good about their future.

CHRIS WASHBURN: "Everybody was excited about the future and were looking to next year because we had a lot of guys coming back, and we had some good talent coming in. I was depressed because that was the last time I was ever going to play with Nate (McMillan). I had wanted to play with Nate ever since I played against him at the Fork Union Military Academy. It was depressing because the next year the locker room was gonna be different. I knew I would have to take on more of a leadership role. At that point, I was definitely coming back."

It had been an incredible year for the Wolfpack. They had over-achieved and almost made it to the Final Four. With Washburn and several other players believed to be coming back, NC State was expecting to have a banner next year. Or, at least, that was the plan.

4

THE DRAFT

"The coaches were in panic mode when they found out I missed my exams. They wanted to know why. Of course I couldn't tell them. I would have to attend summer school, they told me. I may miss the first part of the season of basketball. It was a real mess." ~ Chris Washburn

A month after the NCCA tournament, the North Carolina State University basketball program received a stunner. Chris Washburn would not return to school to play his junior year of basketball.

CHRIS WASHBURN: "I had every intention of coming back to school. I was proud of the season I just had. It was a big turnaround. I was starting to be the face of the team going into that next year. I kind of liked that role."

Without telling the program, Washburn had quietly applied as a hardship case. Valvano received word about the decision through Washburn's mother, Savannah.

CHRIS WASHBURN: "I was nineteen, about to turn twenty. I was still a little immature. Why didn't I tell coach? I didn't want to let anybody down. The fact is, I was afraid to tell coach Valvano that I was leaving school. He was so looking forward to me coming back."

Wolfpack coach Ray Martin, who was at NC State from 1980 to 1988, said he was not surprised that Washburn had decided to turn pro.

RAY MARTIN: "He didn't play that much for us his freshman year, and we knew he was going to go pro eventually because he just was too good to stay around for four years."

But coach Valvano and his coaching staff supported Washburn.

RAY MARTIN: "We all supported Chris. And he was trying to get a better life for him and his family, his mom and dad. I was a little surprised but supportive."

The press tried to reach Washburn at his home in Hickory, North Carolina, but his mother said he was away conducting business.

CHRIS WASHBURN: "Yeah, I had said I was planning to return to NC State. But I also said I was leaving my options open."

Dereck Whittenburg, Washburn's Wolfpack teammate and minder, was not surprised by Washburn's decision, although he found out about it, like everyone else, from newspaper accounts.

DERECK WHITTENBURG: "I really believe that if I would have stayed with Chris, we would've kept on a straight and narrow path. He didn't have anybody around him advising him what to do, to tell him he shouldn't do that or what you should do. He was just a young kid, and everybody on the team was older than him. He didn't really fit in. He was on his own."

To be eligible for the NBA draft, Washburn had to submit a letter requesting a hardship exemption by May 3, 1986, to the NBA Commissioner's office. The draft was set for June 17.

Valvano tried to pose a happy face about Washburn's sudden move. "I can certainly appreciate what Chris has gone through these past two years," Valvano told one reporter. "It was great to see him respond to all the adversity he had to face, and then having a successful sophomore season. I hope he can continue to improve and that he will have an outstanding pro career."

Why the sudden change of mind? He had missed too much school, had to make up too much work, and his playing time for the upcoming season was too uncertain.

Then there was Len Bias. Washburn had met Len Bias in his dormitory room, and his life changed dramatically. Len Bias had come to North Carolina to barnstorm. In basketball, bomb storming is when teams or athletes travel to different locations to play exhibition matches. Bomb-storming teams are different from traveling teams because they don't operate within an established league.

Washburn had met Bias back in January of 1986 when the Wolfpack traveled to the University of Maryland to play in a game that the Wolfpack lost, 67-55.

CHRIS WASHBURN: "I wanted to meet Len. I heard a lot about him. He was a superstar in college basketball. At the University of Maryland, I was directed to a building where he was supposed to be. I saw him walking down the hallway. He stopped and we talked a bit. It was a friendly conversation. Then we went on our separate ways.

"So here he was standing with some other guys at the doorway to my dormitory room. Now I act like a groupie. I'm excited. I invited Len and his boys in. They wanted to use the phone, so I let them. They stayed there for a while, and I could hear them giggling. I had an exam at 7:50 in the morning, so I went to bed.

"When I woke up around six a.m., they were still there. They were all sweating and laughing and having fun. So now I still had a few minutes before I needed to leave, so I sat down with them. Then they pulled this glass jar out. It contained what looked like a rock. They proceeded to light up the rock and smoke it. They would pass the jar back and forth.

"They offered me a hit. I declined, but they kept insisting. They lit the rock for me and told me how to smoke it. I thought it would be like back in the day when somebody offered me marijuana. I took it but never got hooked. This time it was different. I never felt anything like it before. I told the boys: 'did y'all hear that whistle?' They chuckled, and one of the guys asked me: 'do you want to try it again. I took another hit.

"Then a little while later, they said: 'We gotta go to the hotel and get back with the team. We have to play at another city.' We shook hands, and they went on their way.

"My friend C-Lo, who had brought Len and his friends to my room, came back to my room later in the day and told me what it was I had smoked. It was crack cocaine. I was like, where can I get some more of that stuff? The feeling was so good. But then I had to think. I couldn't just go out and ask anybody for it. Everybody knew who I was. I would have to sneak around to find it. Then I would have to cook it myself, and I didn't know how to do that. So I didn't really try crack again until later when I went to play for Golden State."

Meanwhile, the crack experience caused Washburn to miss his exams.

CHRIS WASHBURN: "The coaches were in panic mode when they found out I missed my exams. They wanted to know why. Of course I couldn't tell them. I would have to attend summer school, they told me. I may miss the first part of the season of basketball. It was a real mess."

Not on that day but soon after, Washburn would become another casualty of the new War on Drugs. It would not be heroin or cocaine or methamphetamine or one of the familiar narcotics poisoning America. This time, it would be a far more addicting, insidious drug: crack cocaine.

Crack is made by changing regular powdered cocaine in a basic way. It's really addictive and gives people a big jolt of energy. People get hooked on it because it gives them a fast, intense feeling, and since it's cheap and easy to make, it's easy to find and buy. The significant increase in the use of crack cocaine began in the early 1980s. From the West Coast, the crack cocaine epidemic spread like wildfire across the country. The crack epidemic had particularly devastating effects within the African American communities of the inner cities by causing an increase in addiction, deaths, and drug-related crimes.

CHRIS WASHBURN: "I loved crack day one with that first hit in my dormitory room, but it would be a while before I was hooked on it. I did not want to go to class. Damn! I just wanted another hit to get that feeling. All I thought about was getting my next hit. I would sit around trying to figure out how that could happen.

"I didn't want to go to class. Finally, I left my room and rode around. I traveled to the other side of town where there's a little college called Saint Augustine. It's close to the projects, where a lot of blacks live. I thought I could make a score there. But because I'm so well known, I just couldn't get out of the car and ask people to sell me crack. But eventually, when I began my pro career, I did find crack. But by the time I went to play in the NBA, I was using cocaine. So, I was damaged goods, unprepared, a dope head."

Basketball sources were unaware of Washburn's incipient drug problem, but they questioned whether Washburn was ready to play in the NBA. They acknowledged that he had the talent, physical presence, skill, mobility, and the soft touch to make it the NBA. He definitely had potential.

They pointed out, however, that Washburn had only played ten games in his true freshman year, and, yes, his second year was something to whet the appetite. Still, given his past problems with the law, they questioned his emotional maturity and readiness to handle the grind and temptations of NBA life.

The Boston Celtics legendary president Red Auerbach told the press, "Washburn would have benefited from another year of Jim Valvano's coaching."

Still, despite his misgivings, Auerbach thought that Washburn would go in the top five of the draft. After all, some NBA teams would need a center.

Bob Lipper, a writer for the *Times-Dispatch* newspaper in Richmond, Virginia, wrote that Washburn was an "incomplete player" in many ways. "His intensity fluctuates on the court. As his record suggests—his next coach will be his fifth within a six-year span in case you've lost count. His stability is open to speculation. He's never stayed in one place long enough to let instructions set in or to establish continuity."

Washburn, though, was not paying attention to the nay sayers and their criticism.

CHRIS WASHBURN: "I didn't read the newspapers or pay attention to what the media or the so-called pundits were saying about me. I was focusing on the draft."

The draft itself was not generating a lot of excitement, mainly because it did not include any franchise-making big men. But then suddenly, Washburn and several other underclassmen had decided to leave school and declare for the draft. They included Memphis State center William Bedford, Louisiana State forward John Williams, and former Georgetown forward Michael Graham. These announcements were followed by the surprise announcement of college player of the year Walter Berry. Berry had said that he would stay at St. John's unless he would be the number one pick overall. Then Berry, too, announced that he would make himself eligible for the draft.

So how did Washburn stack up against the other big men entering the draft? Pete Newell, the Golden State Warriors' player personnel director, said of Washburn, "he can block shots. He's a big jumper, but I'm not sure how quick of a jumper. He's got more of a center's body than Bedford or Tarpley, and Daughtery is plenty strong."

Recently, the Warriors had had an abysmal time in the NBA draft. Despite their record, the Warriors did not get the luck of the draw in the 1985 draft and received the seventh pick. But the Warriors management remained optimistic. Newell noted, "This (draft) goes as deep as any draft I can remember."

Once Washburn had decided to turn pro, he knew his first move would be to get an agent to represent him.

CHRIS WASHBURN: "I had an agent's name and number. His name was Larry Gillman. I decided to give him a call to see what he could tell me. I told him I was leaving school and turning pro. Larry said: 'Are you sure about that?' I said, 'Yeah. I am.'

"He said, 'Let me make some calls first because no one in basketball knows that you are leaving college.'"

Gillman made some calls to find out that, if Chris Washburn did leave school, where would he place in the draft? After the first couple of calls, Gillman was told that Washburn could go as high as in the top ten. He relayed that information back to Washburn, but advised, 'don't do anything yet.' He told Washburn that he needed to get more information. He called Washburn back again and said he had spoken with an NBA source who said he could go in the top five.

CHRIS WASHBURN: "Larry told me, 'The information I've giving to you is confidential. Are you sure you want to go?' The information he had provided me with had made me excited. I was more determined than ever to make the move. I told him, 'Yeah. I'm ready.'

"But this was all new to me. I knew nothing about the NBA. I didn't know the players. Didn't know anything about the teams on the East Coast or the West Coast. Didn't know where Golden State was. I didn't know any of that kind of stuff."

Soon after talking with Gillman, Washburn left NC State, took a cab to the airport, and flew to New York.

CHRIS WASHBURN: "I left my room unlocked. No one knew I was going.

I flew to New York and the South Bronx. Then Valvano found out I was planning to leave school. But he or anybody else could find me. In New York I spent a lot of time at the gym at 183rd and Webster. That is where all the top players came to…guys like Scooter McCray, who played for the Rockets and Gus Williams who played for the Washington Wizards, and his brother Ray. Jackie Knowles knew all the players. Jackie was a good player for his time, but later he got black balled from the NBA. And then you had other guys like Gary Springer and Richie Adams. All those guys were like park legends in New York. Many could have gone pro but didn't for whatever reason. Drugs were involved with many of them.

"After my encounter with Len in my dorm room I didn't do any more crack until I came back from Golden State's training camp in Santa Barbara. Never touched it in New York. Now, like I said, when I was in New York City, I was the youngest one in my circle. I was dealing with guys maybe in their early thirties, men who were much older than me.

"And the thing for me was doing powder cocaine. It wasn't like smoking for them or anything like that because if you smoke crack at the time, you were considered a dope fiend.

"But I liked cocaine. Where can I get some more, I wanted to know? They said, 'We got some. You wanna try it?' And, you know, man, I tried it. At first, I tried a little bit, but it really didn't do anything for me yet. It wasn't like the crack I smoked with Len. After maybe about five minutes, the high kicked in. But it was not like the crack high I experienced with Len.

"I went back to the guy and said, 'Look, can you get me some more of that cocaine?' He said, 'How much do you want?' I said, 'give me $500' worth.'

"And this was the way it went in New York. We guys would get together. We would sit around the table and snort cocaine all night. And then those guys would get up from the table and go to work. They all had upper-level jobs."

Draft selection day came on May 7 at the Grand Hyatt Hotel in New York City at approximately 11 a.m. during the halftime of the Philadelphia-Milwaukee playoff game. The last three years of the draft, the selection of the number one pick—Ralph Sampson, Hakeem Olajuwon and Patrick Ewing—was known before draft day. This year, however, who would go number one was a big mystery.

The Philadelphia 76ers and Boston Celtics were the last two teams to have their logos picked out of the sealed envelopes. When the last envelope was opened, it was the 76ers who won the right to pick first. Following Philadelphia and Boston were the four teams in the lottery which did not make the ongoing playoffs—Golden State, Indiana, New York, and Phoenix, respectively. Dallas, a third playoff team, would pick seventh and Cleveland would pick eighth. The 76ers got their first pick in 1979 when the Los Angeles Clippers traded its 1986 pick for Joe Bryant.

Philadelphia could not be more pleased. It had a 54-28 record, the fourth-best in the NBA Eastern Conference. The Celtics did even better. The team had a 67-15 record the past season, the best record in the league. Yet, the Celtics would be picking second because of a trade it made with Seattle in 1984.

No one knew who Philadelphia would pick. "We got a month to figure it out," 76ers executive Pat Williams told the press. "We need size, and we also have the option to trade. If you polled any five NBA executives, (Brad) Daughterty would probably be the front runner. Daughtery is a fail proof pick."

With its number three pick, the Golden State Warriors, in need of a big man, had a good selection from which to choose: Chris Washburn, Memphis State Center William Bedford, or Maryland forward Len Bias.

George Karl, Golden State coach, had this prophetic assessment of Washburn: "He's a combination of size and talent. The most talented player in the draft. Experience and maturity have been questions and could slow his progress early in his career."

 Karl, named head coach of the Montana Golden Nuggets of the Continental Basketball Association, guided the team to the CBA Finals in 1981 and 1983, and won Coach of the Year honors both seasons. Despite the success on the court, the franchise folded in 1983.

In 1983, Karl was working as director of player acquisition with the Cleveland Cavaliers when head coach Tom Nissalke was fired after the season in May 1984. Karl, then 33, was promoted to head coach in late July. In his first season, the Cavaliers made the playoffs for the first time in six seasons. Karl was dismissed by the Cavaliers in mid-March after a disappointing 25–42 start. For the next two months, he was a scout and adviser to the Milwaukee Bucks.[3]

Around the end of May 1986, Karl became the coach of the Golden State Warriors. He turned the team around, taking them from a losing season to making it into the playoffs, something they hadn't done in a whole decade.

Washburn and Karl would not get along.

---

3. "George Karl," Wikipedia, January 29, 2025, https://en.wikipedia. org/wiki/George_Karl.

CHRIS WASHBURN: "We got along okay at first, but, eventually, I didn't really care for him. He was always riding me."

Before the draft, Washburn was invited to attend various NBA pre-season camps.

CHRIS WASHBURN "I started traveling around and trying out for different teams before the draft. But at the same time, I would do cocaine. I would stop doing cocaine, go workout and then after practice, do the cocaine all over again. I wasn't actually hooked on cocaine at this time. I could work out without any kind of physical problems.

"When I got a call to come to Golden State, I went up against some of the team's second-string players: Rod Higgins, Ben McDonald, and Jerome White. I had the speed to go around them. I had the strength to play against the forwards. I had a good showing. Then we would come back to New York, and we would celebrate, you know, with more cocaine."

It was remarkable that Washburn was keeping up this double life: basketball player by day, druggie at night. Nobody was catching on to the Washburn hidden life. Karl would later explain the Washburn dilemma: hard-working player on the court. Off the court, wondering when the next negative phone call about Washburn would be.

CHRIS WASHBURN: "We got more calls, including one from Cleveland, but we thought they'd take Brad Daugherty, and we turned them down. That just gave me more time to snort cocaine and that's what we did. Then we got an offer to come to Boston. My agent found out the Celtics had just given Larry Bird a new contract of $1,000,000. My agent said we could do better than that. So, we turned them down. Philadelphia never asked me to come out, but I thought they would pick me number one."

The day before the draft, the rumor had it that Golden State would be choosing guard Ron Harper as their number 3 pick. The 6'6" guard was Mid-American Conference Player of the Year, averaging 24.4 points a game.

Eight teams watched as NBA commissioner David Stern broke open seven envelopes and decided the order for the 1986 draft, which would take place on June 17.

On Monday, June 16, in the early afternoon, Len Bias arrived in New York City with his father, James, in preparation for the NBA draft. They stayed at the Grand Hyatt at league expense. At 1 p.m. that day, the NBA held a news conference with Brad Daugherty, Johnny Dawkins, Pearl Washington, John Salley, Walter Berry, and Kenny Walker attending. Bias did not attend.

Two hours later, the NBA had an orientation session conducted by Tom Saunders, Paul Silas, and Trent Tucker to explain to the players the Draft Day process. Washburn and many of the top draft choices attended, but Bias did not. At 6:30 that evening, an informal buffet dinner was held for about fifty guests, with league commissioner David Stern, front office personnel from the league, and friends and family of the players attending.

Washburn had been partying with his pals with cocaine, but he was excited about going to the draft and experiencing the glitz and glamor of the event.

On Tuesday, the following day, at 10 a.m., the players attending the draft checked out of the hotel and had breakfast together at the Grand Hyatt. The players, including Chris Washburn, were driven to the Felt Forum, where the draft would be conducted.

Chris Washburn had prepared for the draft.

CHRIS WASHBURN: "I went shopping and bought three designer suits, each one costing $3500. I still remember the name of the designer: Carl Davis. I went shopping for cars. I was doing the things I needed to do. And at night I was getting high on cocaine."

When he showed up at the Grand Hyatt Hotel for the draft, Washburn was stoned. But he noticed that some of the other attendee athletes were as well. Washburn waited bleary-eyed and with anticipation for his name to be called. NBA team reps watched anxiously as the selection began.

A crowd of 1,857 fans in the darkened Coliseum Area applauded after Brad Daughtery and Len Bias were selected as the first two picks by Philadelphia and Boston. Cleveland had picked up the number one pick in a trade with Philadelphia. The draft picks were greeted by Stern on stage and conducted interviews with reporters.

The crowd cheered Golden State's decision to select Washburn as the third player in the draft. Golden State did not commit to Washburn until 7:30 Monday night, the day before, after reviewing film of Washburn and its other two possible choices, Len Bias and Ron Harper. George Karl revealed that he had never done as much research in selecting Washburn and that, of the three, Washburn was the most "exciting."

The consensus of opinion, however, was that Golden State's choice of Washburn was a big risk. The press wanted to know about Washburn's criminal record. Karl downplayed Washburn's past indiscretions, describing Washburn's legal scraps as "pranks." Karl conceded that Washburn had been "irresponsible" off the court, but vowed to give Washburn the attention he needed to help him behave.

CHRIS WASHBURN: "Yeah, my pick was controversial, but I was happy with it. I went to San Franscico, played against a few of the guys. The area was nice. The weather was nice. I had met a couple of girls. The reception they gave me was warm. Even for the short time I was out there I liked it."

In the past Golden State had had problems signing their number one picks. But Golden State management said it planned to get Washburn under contract quickly. Golden State wanted to team Washburn with seven-foot Joe Barry Carroll, a partnership coach Karl described as the "Golden State Twin Towers."

The scrutiny of Washburn in the press continued. Given Washburn's past, much of the league had questions about the young prodigy and whether he had truly changed. Was he ready to play in the NBA and avoid problems? But for Washburn, there were no doubts.

CHRIS WASHBURN: "I had no doubts that I would make it in the NBA. It would take a few years, but I would eventually become one of the best big men in the league."

On draft day, June 17, Washburn was disappointed about not being picked number one, but he congratulated Bias on being picked second. Bias told Washburn that he would be in Washington on June 19 at a party and asked if he wanted to come. Washburn told Bias that he would be driving back to North Carolina in the new Mercedes he had bought in New York City and would stop by. They clasped hands and went on their way.

After the draft, Bias left for Boston accompanied by his father, a Celtics' team representative and Bill Shelton, a representative of Advantage International, the Washington-based firm that represents Bias. At 4:30 p.m., the group arrived at Logan International Airport in Boston, and Bias was met by the local media.

From six to seven p.m., Bias appeared on all three local television news shows, one of which featured a live interview. "It's been a long day and I've been talking to a lot of guys," Bias said of his day with the media.

On Wednesday late morning, Bias traveled to Avon, Massachusetts, where he signed a long-term endorsement contract with Reebok sportswear. In the early evening, Bias attended dinner with Reebok executives, and Celtics guard Danny Ainge at the Royal Sonesta Hotel in Cambridge, Massachusetts.

At 7:30 that night, Bias left Boston's Logan International Airport on a flight bound for Washington, D.C. After arriving in Washington, Bias headed to his family's home in Landover, Maryland, a Washington suburb.

At approximately 11:30 p.m. that night, Bias left his home in his newly purchased Nissan 300ZX sports car to return to Washington Hall, his dormitory on the campus of the University of Maryland in College Park. Bias socialized with a group of friends, including Terrapins' teammates, in the dormitory. At 2 a.m., Thursday morning, Bias said he wanted to be alone, and he left the dorm in his car. He headed for a small party off-campus.

An hour later, Bias returned to his dorm room and continued talking with his friends, including teammates David Gregg, Terry Long and Keith Gatlin. Approximately five hours later, Bias collapsed on his couch while talking with the friends. Efforts to revive him with cardio-pulmonary resuscitation failed. An ambulance arrived at 6:32 p.m.

Soon after, Prince George's County fire department ambulance, paramedic unit, and fire engine responded to a report of 'a man not breathing' and found friends administering CPR to Bias in his dorm room. Unconscious,

Bias was taken to Leland Memorial Hospital emergency room in nearby Riverdale.

Frantic efforts were made to save Bias. Doctors injected him with five different drugs, including adrenaline, in an effort to resuscitate him. After chemicals failed to work, a pacemaker was implanted in his heart muscle in an attempt to get the heart going again by electrical shock.

It was too late. All rescue efforts failed. At 8:50 a.m., on June 19, Len Bias was pronounced dead.

Washburn was still in New York walking down the street, when someone recognized him and asked, "Hey, man, did you hear about Len Bias?

Washburn asked, "What about Len?"

The man said, "Len's dead."

The news shook Washburn. He bought a newspaper from a nearby newsstand and read the story. Incredulously, it was true.

CHRIS WASHBURN: "I thought: Len can't be dead. I had seen him at the draft. He looked so healthy. I learned from the newspaper that they suspected it was a cocaine overdose. I was sick. I had been doing coke. That's all I've been doing since I came to New York. Damn! It could have been me. I felt embarrassed. I didn't want anybody to know that Len gave me my first hit."

Five days later, Dr. John Smialek, the Maryland state medical examiner, determined Len Bias had died of cocaine intoxication. Smialek said Bias was killed by a jolt of cocaine he had probably snorted only minutes before he collapsed in his dorm room. Smialek said the cocaine interrupted the electrical activity in Bias's brain, causing the heart to begin to beat irregularly. Speaking at a news conference, Dr.

Smialek said, "There were no signs that he drank alcohol or consumed other drugs on the night of his death."

In the autopsy, Smialek also noted that "Bias was in otherwise good health and was not suffering from any heart condition that might have contributed to his passing."[4]

"This resulted in the sudden onset of seizures and cardiac arrest," Smialek determined. The latest conclusions from the autopsy report came on a day when University of Maryland Chancellor John B. Slaughter acknowledged that he was briefed last week by federal drug agents about an undercover investigation that spilled over onto the Maryland campus.

On July 25, 1986, a grand jury indicted Brian Tribble, a friend of Len Bias, for possessing cocaine with the intent to distribute. Bias's Maryland teammates, Terry Long, and David Gregg, were also charged with cocaine possession and obstruction of justice. As a result, Long and Gregg were suspended from the team on July 31. In August, all three defendants pleaded not guilty.

On October 20, the charges against Long and Gregg were dropped in exchange for their testimony against Tribble. Then, on October 30, the grand jury issued three additional indictments against Tribble, including one for conspiracy to obstruct justice and two for obstruction of justice. Ultimately, on June 3, 1987, Tribble was acquitted of all charges related to the Bias case.[5]

Did Chris Washburn learn anything from the Len Bias tragedy?

---

4. Lorenzo Tanos, "Disturbing Details Found in Len Bias' Autopsy Report," Grunge, April 22, 2022, https://www.grunge.com/840759/disturbing-details-found-in-len-bias-autopsy-report/.

5. "Len Bias," Wikipedia, March 9, 2025, https://en.wikipedia.org/wiki/Len_Bias.

CHRIS WASHBURN: "Len's death affected me, sure, and I thought about it long and hard. In the back of my mind, I really knew it could have been me. But it didn't change my behavior."

Washburn would continue pursuing his lifestyle on the edge. His life was becoming like a ticking time bomb that was bound to explode. It was just a matter of time.

5

GREAT EXPECTATIONS

"Sure, I was happy because I would be playing basketball again. But the money really didn't faze me. Money was always present in my life. All I had to do was go to the bank and get money. I never had to pay bills or anything like that because the agent and his agency took care of it." ~ Chris Washburn

After draft day, June 19, 1986, nothing was heard from Chris Washburn for a day and a half. Even Washburn's father, Dwight Washburn, said he did not know his son's whereabouts. Finally, Washburn appeared, telling the press that he had been in the Bronx, New York, officiating youth charity games. It would be the first of many unpredictable events during Washburn's tenure with Golden State.

Five days later, Washburn appeared at his first Bay area press conference. Washburn, barely 20, showed up dressed like a GQ magazine model, wearing a dark gray silk suit, white collar shirt, and stylish tie and looking like the hot shot high NBA draft choice who would soon sign a contract making him a millionaire.

"When a big man goes out," Washburn told the gathering, "People are always looking at him. So, I have to have on something different."

The press wanted to know when Washburn would begin practicing with the Warriors. Larry Gillman, his agent, had been insistent that Washburn not play in the rookie camp that extended from July 12th to July 24th unless his client was under contract. The Warriors had offered to buy Washburn a million-dollar insurance policy to guard against a potential career-ending injury. Gillman had rejected the offer, stating that why mess around with an insurance policy when they can go right ahead and work out a contract. Washburn assured the media that when he did sign, he would be ready to play.

Washburn was expected to play in the new NBA/Charlotte Pro-Am Summer League. The league started five years previously as a development league for referees but had gone from a five-city operation its first summer to a twenty-city operation in 1986. Washburn was to join some rising young NBA stars that included Michael Jordan of the Chicago Bulls and Bob McAdoo of the Philadelphia 76ers. In the end, Washburn did not participate, given his agent's concern that he might get injured, thus potentially jeopardizing Washburn's contract negotiations.

Washburn did not sign with the Warriors until September 12, three weeks before the start of the Warriors' training camp. Gillman met with Dan Finnane, the Warriors' president, face to face in New York City to hammer out the deal. Finnane had recently purchased the club along with Jim Fitzgerald, and the partners were hoping to move the Warriors in a new direction after failing to make the playoffs the past nine years. Finnane wanted to avoid the kind of fiasco the previous draft had caused with Chris Mullin, last year's number-one pick, when he missed training camp and the first seven games of the regular season.

Washburn became the first first-round draft choice to sign with the Warriors before the start of training camp since 1978, when the club signed two first rounders, Purvis Short and Ray Townsend. Although details of the deal were not disclosed, it was believed to be worth $3.5 million for four years. Despite Washburn's unproven status, the deal was completely guaranteed.

Overnight, Washburn had become a very rich and a very happy young man. Agent Gillman beamed at a press conference, "I think I had a pretty good feel for what is being offered to the other top picks, what kind of money was available." Gillman told the *San Jose Mercury News,* "My job was to get job security for Chris Washburn, and we got four years totally guaranteed."

Washburn took signing the contract in stride.

CHRIS WASHBURN: "Sure, I was happy because I would be playing basketball again. But the money really didn't faze me. Money was always present in my life. All I had to do was go to the bank and get money. I never had to pay bills or anything like that because the agent and his agency took care of it.

"I did get a tiny amount of bonus money. I bought my mom a car. I bought my dad a truck. I told my mom to go and start looking for a house. I felt good about doing something for my parents before buying anything for myself. But I went ahead and bought a mansion up in the hills of Oakland where a lot of other athletes, baseball players, and entertainers lived. I also bought myself a car, a Mercedes SEL 500. I had all the stuff taken out, and I put in a Rolls Royce interior and an upgraded stereo system. The car was valued at about

$180,000. That was back in the eighties. It would probably be worth half a mil today."

Washburn indicated that he planned to be in the Bay area the next two or three weeks to prepare for the opening of training camp on October 3 in Santa Barbara, California. Washburn said he had been working out and claimed to be in the best shape of his life.

Washburn, however, was having trouble adjusting to life in the NBA. He was a lot younger than the other players and had a hard time fitting in.

CHRIS WASHBURN: "I was a young kid far away from friends, family, and home. I felt kinda pressured to try and find somebody who I could relate to and who would look out for me. I was expecting the players to be more friendly, that they would come around and get to know me. That's how you build relationships. It wasn't like that, though, in the NBA back then. All my teammates have been together for some years, and I'm a new guy coming in trying to take somebody's position. I thought we were all on the same team, but, again, I never really knew anything about the NBA and how it worked.

"I was an only child who had no brother or sister to guide me. I didn't have anybody to talk to. I was lonely. But I saw that if I had cocaine or could buy it, I could attract people to me. I could sit and talk to those people, and they would listen… or, to be honest, probably not listen."

Washburn's NBA career started off on a shaky note on October 12 in his first game as a Warrior. He scored ten points and grabbed seven rebounds off the bench but made only four of sixteen shot attempts in the Warrior victory over the Sacramento Kings. Teammate Larry Smith described Washburn's play as 'jumping around, swinging his elbows," quipping that "swinging your elbows at that position will get you a new set of dentures."

Yet, despite Washburn's loneliness and his casual drug use, his play with the Warriors started off well. On October 15, he scored sixteen points and hauled in nine rebounds against the Knicks. He excited the crowd with some offensive moves and artistic baskets. The Knicks routed the Warriors 117-84 in what was a disappointing loss for the Warriors.

Washburn continued his promising play on October 20 when the Warriors rebounded for a 97-84 victory over the New York Knicks. Washburn came off the bench in the second quarter to score thirteen points and give the Warriors a 54-45 lead. He scored on an amazing three-point play while he was going in for a dunk. He adjusted in mid-air and dropped a layup. Fouled, he converted a free throw to give the Warriors a 35-29 lead.

Washburn had the flu in Golden State's close 107-105 victory over the Los Angeles Lakers, which probably helped explain his poor performance in the Warriors' next game, a 114-102 loss to the New Jersey Nets. In a reserve role, Washburn made three of four free-throw attempts to finish with five points.

Washburn continued to play well in his next game, leading the Warriors in their 114-108 loss to the New York Knicks with an impressive twenty-three points. Washburn's performance was so impressive, in fact, that there was talk of him replacing Larry Smith at power forward. Washburn had played backup center so far in the pre-season because coach Karl thought playing Washburn and Joe Bob Carroll together would hurt the team's fast break. But in their next exhibition game, the pre-season finale against Seattle in Boseman, Montana, Washburn started ahead of Larry Smith.

Washburn had gotten off to a promising start in his NBA career, but that did not seem to help him with his relationship with coach George Karl. There was friction between them from the get-go.

CHRIS WASHBURN: "We really didn't see eye to eye. I felt he was always on top of me. It never seemed like I could be good enough for him. There was some competition there, too. We both played in the ACC, he with the (University of North Carolina (Tar Heels) and me with the Wolfpack. He was staunchly Tar Heels and would constantly be talking about them. It got tiresome. I would tell him, 'Coach that was another era.' I don't think he liked that. It wasn't fun playing for him."

At first, Washburn would practice and play basketball in the daytime while at night cruising Oakland to see what was out there. As we said, Oakland at the time had a negative reputation as a city infested with crime, gangs, and drug dealing. The Warriors management warned its players to be careful when they moved and mixed in Oakland.

As in many other American cities during the 1980s, crack cocaine had become a serious problem in Oakland. Drug dealing in general, and the dealing of crack cocaine in particular, resulted in elevated rates of violent crime, causing Oakland to consistently be listed as one of America's most crime-ridden cities. Oakland's murder rate rose two times that of San Francisco or New York City during the late 1980's, and the city was regularly listed as one of the U.S. cities most plagued by crime.

CHRIS WASHBURN: "When I came to San Francisco, I was a young guy with a lot of energy, but I was depressed being away from friends and family. I found the NBA to be totally different from college. It was difficult to make friends. I wanted to get out in the evening and do some things, meet some people. So, I had to do it basically on my own. In the evenings, I would go to sleep, then I'd wake up around 12 or 1 o'clock at night. Having the energy, I would leave the house and start cruising.

"The first night, after we came back from training camp at Santa Barbara, I went out on the town trying to be as discreet as I could driving my $180,000 Mercedes. I rode deep into the projects. I cruised around and saw somebody standing on a corner. I could tell the guy was hustling. I flagged him down. He came over to my car. I asked him where I could get some coke. He said he had it, but he would have to go somewhere to get it. I said, 'Okay, here is $500.' He told me he would have to go somewhere to get the dope. He went around the corner, and I never saw him again. I was new to the game. I had been stiffed.

"But I didn't get upset. Luckily, I had a lot of money on me. I found another person and said to him, 'Here is $300. Can you get me some dope?' He said 'Yeah, brother, let me get it for you.' This time, I told him this time that I wouldn't give him the money unless I had the dope in hand because somebody had ripped me off.

"So, when he came back with the dope, we exchanged the money for the crack, I drove off. I found a house where I could do the dope. Then I had no dope. I had $100 left. I said, "Look here. I got a $100. Can you find us something?" He said, 'yeah, man.'

"I was sitting in this person's house, so I knew he had to come back if I gave him the money. He eventually came back with some dope. It was around 3, 3:30, in the morning, maybe a quarter to four. So, we started getting high. Knowing that I had to practice at 10 AM the next morning, I smoked all the way up to about 9 or 9:15. Then I went to practice. I was wide awake.

"Nobody at the practice suspected anything. Coach Karl wanted me to do some additional workouts, so, I did them. Then I went home, changed clothes, and got something to eat. I kept going back to the projects, smoking crack. I would go late at night so people wouldn't see me. I would give them the money, and they would bring back the crack.

"This is my first experience with crack since I did it with Bias. It was a much stronger high. It was a different high. It was a quicker high. Just as soon as I took the smoke in and blew it out, I was high, whereas in the case of the powder cocaine, it would take you a few minutes to get high. Smoking crack let me escape. Let me sit back. Let me feel like I was the king of the hill.

"Now I'm starting to get comfortable in California. I was doing this most days, smoking crack and playing ball. I might meet a girl at the game, and we might go out to dinner or something like that, but most nights, I'm in the projects in East Oakland, getting high."

The 1986-87 NBA opened on October 30 with Golden State predicted to be the only challenger to the Los Angeles Lakers in the league's weakest division. The Warriors had the talent, with Purvis Short, Joe Barry Carroll, and Sleepy Floyd leading the way. Larry Smith and Jerome Whitehead were considered competent inside players, but given the recent play of Washburn, they were expected to lose minutes to the talented freshman player. The experts predicted that Washburn would have to have a stellar season. He needed it if the Warriors were to be successful.

Coach Karl was optimistic. "Our goal is to make the playoffs for the first time in eight or nine years," he told the press.

The Warriors' first game on November 1 was a disappointing loss to the Phoenix Suns at Phoenix, 127-123. The Warriors could have easily folded, but they battled back before falling short. Washburn's contribution was modest. He played nineteen minutes and had seven points.

The Warriors began a three-game homestay three days later with a comfortable win over the New York Knicks, 104-95. Karl benched Washburn, inserting Larry Smith in his place. Critics pointed out that the lack of rebounding was a major problem for the team. In its first three games, the Warriors had lost the boards by an average of 48.3 to 44.3 rebounds. Bill Sullivan, a writer with the *Mercury News,* criticized Washburn's rebounding deficiencies as coming down to one problem: "too often he simply doesn't jump."

Washburn was beginning to have personal problems. He had missed a weight training session at the Shape Clinic in Oakland. It was the second problem in less than a week for Washburn. He had previously missed practice and received a fine. Karl downplayed Washburn's infractions, attributing them simply to a "breakdown in communication."

On November 12, the Warriors were humiliated, losing to the Portland Trail Blazers 126-108 for their twenty-seventh loss in twenty-eight games at Portland. Karl criticized his team for its lack of energy and lackadaisical play. Washburn replaced Carroll in the game but lasted only two minutes on the court after Portland's Steve Johnson beat him badly on two plays.

Washburn's problems continued to mount. He made the news when he missed a practice by driving one-third of the way to Sacramento while trying to get from San Francisco to Oakland.

CHRIS WASHBURN: "I was so stoned. I was using more and more crack. I couldn't stop smoking. I got confused. I got lost. It was embarrassing."

Before that experience, however, Washburn had showed up late for a team bus in Boston. Then he turned up 25 minutes late after he was supposed to be at Madison Square Garden for another game against the New York Knicks.

CHRIS WASHBURN: "Basketball had become my second job, not the first. My first job was getting high. I was losing interest in basketball. I was up at night, two nights in a row, smoking crack. I started missing practice or I would come in late and get fined. I would get fined $5,000 to $10,000 per offense. It seemed like a lot of money, but the money never seemed to run out. I would go to the bank on a Friday and take out $15,000. By the next Monday, I would show at the bank again to withdraw more money." At the height of his crack habit, Washburn estimates he was blowing about $17,000 a month.

CHRIS WASHBURN: "I would come to practice not really interested in playing basketball, but just wanting to finish up so I could get high. Getting fined didn't make any difference."

Remarkably, Washburn still managed to help the Warriors to win. When the Warriors beat the Knicks 97-93, Washburn thrilled the crowd with an awesome follow-up slam of a Ben McDonald miss. Washburn played thirteen minutes and had six points.

Still, Karl was frustrated with Washburn's behavior, complaining in the press that Washburn's tardiness and recent actions were "irresponsible." The press revealed that Washburn had been fined at least four times previously for being late on opening night in Oakland, missing practice while in route to the state capital, being inattentive at practice, and failing to show up for his weight-training session.

Washburn had an excuse for each infraction. He got tied up with relatives. He was visiting family in the Bronx and lost track of time. He claimed to have told the team trainer that he would miss the bus but be at the Boston Gardens at 7 pm. Washburn told the press he would explain things to coach Karl.

By this time, the Warriors were getting an inkling of what Washburn was doing with his free time. No one had actually seen Washburn with a dope dealer or buying crack, but it was hard to miss his expensive Mercedes when it showed up in the projects.

CHRIS WASHBURN: "The Warriors management would let me know that they had seen my car at such and such a place in such and such area. Management would then get in touch with my talent agency and tell them that I've been hanging in places I shouldn't be. Someone needs to talk to me."

It was revealed after the Knicks game that teammate Greg Ballard had been appointed as a kind of big brother to Washburn. Ballard was a 10-year veteran with three kids of his own. His responsibilities in minding Washburn were to make sure that he was supposed to be on time and to act like a big brother.

Karl had gathered his team around him one day and asked, "Who's going to take care of the rook. Who's going to take charge?" Ballard volunteered for the job.

CHRIS WASHBURN: "What made the arrangement hard on Greg was that Karl told him that anytime I'm late or I didn't show up where I was supposed to be, not only would I get fined, but he's gonna get fined as well. Ballard would get panicky when he couldn't find me or when I was not where I was supposed to be."

It was understandable then why Ballard was not too happy with being Washburn's big brother. He went public with his frustrations. He was seen before one game, animated, giving Washburn a lecture. After the game, Ballard blasted Washburn, telling the press, "Your job comes first. Your relatives have to understand that. It's just a matter of taking pride in what you do."

Ballard noted that Washburn had a four-year, $3 million contract and suggested that "They (the Warriors) ought to take a big bundle of cash, stick it in his pocket, then pull it back out. Then he'll know what he's missing."

Under the coaching of first-year coach George Karl, the Warriors were proving to be the early surprise of the West. Washburn's play, however, had not contributed to the Warriors good start. Washburn's stats at this point of the season were not impressive. He was averaging 3.2 points and 4.2 rebounds per game and shooting 36.7 percent from the free throw line and 31.8 percent from the field. Frustrating the Warriors was the fact that Washburn would show flashes of the talent that seemed to justify the Warriors picking him third in the 1986 draft, such as a seventeen-point, twelve-rebound performance against the Lakers. In terms of his talent, Washburn was not disappointing. It was just a question of his motivation and attitude.

Washburn's poor performance and nonchalant and indifferent demeanor helped wear out his welcome in the Warriors locker room. His teammates wondered what was going on with the team's prize rookie and why he hadn't been suspended.

Coach Karl seemed to have endless patience, but he was concerned about how Washburn's rule-breaking behavior was affecting the team. He admitted that he had considered suspending Washburn and hitting him where it hurt financially by enforcing the conduct clause in his contract.

Then in early December, Greg Ballard gave up his role of big brother. The final straw was Washburn being late three times in four days. No need to worry on the Warriors part. In Ballard's place came Jackie Knowles, the 34-year-old former basketball player at Niagara University, who worked for Gus Williams Enterprises, the company that represented Washburn. Knowles and Washburn had become close friends the previous summer when Washburn played ball in Webster Police Athletic League in the South Bronx, where Knowles was athletic director.

Knowles planned to stay with Washburn when the Warriors played at home, but he would return to New York while the Warriors were on road trips. Knowles said he was not worried about assuming the role of Washburn's minder. He noted that he had been a minder to a lot of teams in New York and had been like a father or mother to many a young baller.

Knowles was upbeat about his arrival in San Francisco to help out the Warriors with their troubled prodigy. "Chris is a big fun-loving kid," Knowles told the press. "People have always catered to Chris. No one had ever laid a hand on him. When you get smacked down after that, you don't believe it the first few times."

The Warriors, now worried and desperate about Washburn's behavior and playing status, welcomed Knowles's move. Warriors President Finanne said of the arrangement, "It's no surprise. With a young guy so far from home. I welcome it."

The Washburn-Knowles relationship was off to a good start after Knowles arrived; Washburn was on the court ten minutes before a practice session began before a December 4 game against the Houston Rockets. Prior to the Rockets game, Washburn had been kept out of the Warriors last three games. It was a big change from the beginning of the season, a little more than a month ago when Washburn had started the first two games of the season.

Eventually, Knowles had to get back to his job and Washburn was left without a big brother. That's when Washburn's uncle, Ted Hodge, came aboard.

CHRIS WASHBURN: "I convinced my mother's brother to quit his job and come out and live with me. My uncle worked for Payne Weber in Boston, Massachusetts, but after twenty-five years, he quit the company. But I didn't know that he had a cocaine problem. That was not good. After he came out to live with me, he started smoking crack as well. A lot of times, when my car was seen in places where I was not supposed to be, it wasn't me. It was him. And I would get accused of it."

After Washburn was traded from Golden State to Atlanta, Hodge came to live with Washburn. He stayed with him until Washburn was banned from the league.

Golden State became so concerned with Washburn's health that they eventually employed the famous Harry Edwards as a kind of sports psychologist for Washburn for a brief period. Edwards is an American sociologist and civil rights activist who worked as a professor of sociology at the University of California, Berkeley. Edwards's career focused on the experiences of African American athletes. Edwards worked with the Golden State Warriors 1987 through 1995, specializing in player personnel recruitment and counseling.

CHRIS WASHBURN: "At that time, I hardly knew anything about Harry Edwards. I just knew he was some important Black guy who was involved in civil rights. We talked a few times, but it didn't help that much."

On December 14, in a game with the San Antonio Spurs, Washburn was put on the Warriors Do Not Play list, the second straight game that had happened. In Washburn's place, Karl chose Jerome Whitehead, who was given twenty-one minutes in each game. What was going on with the Warriors and with Chris Washburn? Karl downplayed the move, attributing it to the good play of other players.

Yet speculation abounded about how coach Karl and the Warriors had had it with Washburn. Karl had spent months trying to get their troubled rookie to shape up and be a productive member of the team. Coach Karl had essentially been treating Washburn with kid gloves, hoping that somehow, he would come around and shape up.

Washburn's behavior was affecting the team. There were grumblings from Washburn's teammates about the divide that appeared to exist between Washburn's behavior on the one hand and that of his teammates on the other. Now, it appeared, Karl was making Washburn persona non grata.

CHRIS WASHBURN: "I missed practice a couple of times that week, and it ticked off the management. They had a pretty good idea I was using, but they didn't seem to know what to do about it. They didn't really talk to me about it. They just put me on the list. I was in denial at the time. I thought I could do crack and play basketball at the same time. I would leave straight from the projects and go to practice or to a game. My heart would be beating really fast from the cocaine. Then I would have to walk into a crowd of twenty-four to twenty-seven thousand people and I'm high. I know I have to perform, so now my heart is beating double fast. The doctors told me that they didn't know how I didn't die on the court.

"Later, when knowledge about my drug use came out, people marveled at why my heart didn't explode while I was on the court, or why I didn't die of a heart attack. The truth was, I didn't want to stop because I enjoyed using too much. I loved the high."

The problems with Washburn did not cease. Washburn was placed on the Warriors injured list in early January 1987. The team provided no public explanation.

Then, suddenly, on January 28, 1987, Washburn voluntarily stepped forward to seek help with his drug problem. Washburn had got a call from his agent, warning him that the NBA was coming out to Oakland to drug test him.

CHRIS WASHBURN "Larry Gillman told me that I had to go to rehab immediately because the NBA people were already on their way to see me. 'If they find you, they'll test you, and if you test positive, you'll be suspended. So, get your stuff together and let's go. You will have to go into treatment.'"

Under the NBA's drug program, players who admit to drug problems and volunteer for treatment are not penalized the first two times the drug problem happens. Players, however, who test positive for drugs without volunteering for treatment are permanently suspended. Washburn's agency picked him up ASAP, and took him to the Treatment Center in Van Nuys, California, for Washburn's treatment. He was expected to be there for a minimum of four weeks.

CHRIS WASHBURN: "So we chartered a helicopter. That's the first time I've ever been on a helicopter. We flew from Oakland to Van Nuys. From there, we took the van to the hospital. I didn't know what to expect. I just knew that I had to be inside of that place so that the NBA couldn't test me at that point in time. We did the paperwork. We had beaten the NBA's drug testing team."

6

RELAPSE AND REHAB

"...Smoking crack let me escape. Let me sit back. Let me feel like I was the king of the hill." ~ Chris Washburn

At the time that Chris Washburn entered rehab, his lack of productivity and decline as a useful member of the Warriors was shocking. In the eight games from late December 1986 to mid-January 1987, he scored a total of paltry four points while playing just twenty-five minutes.

One would think that Washburn would have been eager to get his act together and prove that he belonged in the NBA. Think again.

CHRIS WASHBURN: "When I left rehab, I had already made up my mind I was gonna continue to use drugs when I got out. I wanted to make up for lost time. My team was expecting me to have changed. What they got was the same old Chris. I could tell the team was a little pissed off at me, upset, because they acted different toward me in the practices. Our guys were shooting elbows, trying to push me around. One time, Joe (Barry Carroll) got a rebound, turned around and hit me right in the mouth with his elbow. I had to go and get a root canal done to fix my mouth.

"The team was upset with me 'cause I wouldn't carry my weight. I can understand that now. Back then, though, I was in a depressed state. I was young, without mentors, I couldn't talk with anybody. So, I just kept doing what I was doing."

It did not help that the Warriors management did not reach out to Washburn to talk about the problem.

CHRIS WASHBURN: "Maybe management should have brought me in, maybe not for a formal meeting, but maybe they could have taken me out to dinner, maybe invited me to one of their houses for a talk. Maybe I would have changed if they had done that. We don't really know. 'cause it never happened."

Today, Washburn wonders: what if the great Julius Erving, Dr. J, had become the mentor he needed? That almost happened when Erving's Philadelphia 76ers played the Warriors early in Washburn's rookie season.

CHRIS WASHBURN: "Erving approached me before a game and asked if we could meet afterward at the Sixers' hotel. At the time, I was living in a hotel. Doctor J was at the tail end of his career, but he was still Doctor J. When Erving showed up to meet me, I was high on crack. There was a knock at the door. I got up and went to the door. I looked at Dr. J through a peep hole. Then he left. I never opened the door. Could Dr. J. had been my savior? I will never know. He extended a hand, but I didn't accept it. If we could have met, he might have said something to me or maybe made me wanna do something different to change my life. We'll never know. Later, after I had left basketball and had recovered. I met Dr. J. at a gathering. I apologized for not meeting him that night. He just looked at me, kinda nodded, and walked away."

On January 20, Washburn was hospitalized with a kidney problem that would require extensive tests. Team physician Robert Alto surmised that Washburn could be having a serious medical problem that might require extensive tests. The problem was revealed when Washburn failed a physical for an insurance policy the team wanted to buy for him as a guarantee against his four-year $3 million contract. Coach Karl told the press the problem was not related. Washburn had lost 22 pounds since the NBA season began.

Then coach Karl quietly benched Washburn. Rumors were swirling that Karl and the Warriors management had had it with Washburn's erratic behavior. And now, suddenly, Washburn was in rehab, where he would spend the next fifty-one days in the treatment facility at Van Nuys dealing with his drug habit. Nobody knew, although there was speculation, that Washburn had been forced to enter the treatment program on his own after learning the league had planned to drug test him.

Had Washburn's drug abuse been detected before he came forward on his own, he would have been suspended for a minimum of two years. When released by the treatment center, he would have been able to join the team without suspension. Since this was the first time Washburn had asked for help, he would be paid during his rehabilitation. If he required a second trip to the clinic, he would not be paid. A third time, and he would be suspended from the league.

CHRIS WASHBURN: "For the first few days at the treatment center, I didn't really do anything. All they wanted me to do was eat, rest, and get some sleep. They'd come in and check my heart rate, my vital signs, things like that, making sure I wouldn't have any kind of complications coming off the drugs. At that time, I didn't get involved in any group sessions. But then about the third day, or maybe the fourth, they came in and asked me to come to a group session being held that morning. So, I went to the group session.

"I didn't do anything. There were several groups that I did that with. And then after that, because I was an NBA player, they took me and a couple other NBA guys in the program to the gym where I worked out. Those other NBA guys were Mitchell Wiggins of the Houston Rockets, Derrick Mayfield of the Boston Celtics, and Lewis Lloyd of the Houston Rockets. I kinda hung with them. That's what I did the first couple of weeks. I didn't really miss the crack in the beginning. I was focused on fitting into the program, doing what everybody else was doing.

"After about two weeks, I thought I had made progress, so it was time for me to go, or so I thought. I left the facility. I felt as though I was clean, but they were telling me: you are only fooling yourself. That's the drug calling you out. You're not ready to leave our facility. You just want to get high. I told them: 'No, I'm clean I just want to play basketball.' They wouldn't release me, so I left on my own.

"By chance, I learned one of the visitors to the center was from Hickory, my hometown. He lived in Van Nuys. I called him when I left the facility. He came and picked me up. But this friend loved to get high. So, after I left the facility, for maybe about three days, I was at his house, where we sat around and got high. So, what the doctors at the facility said was true. I wanted to leave the facility to get high.

"Then I decided to come back to the facility, and I started all over again. After going to detox again for about two or three days, I went back to attending the group sessions. It was supposed to be a thirty-day program, but it wasn't for me. I ended up staying a few days.

"I started listening to some of the other patients. They were telling me what I needed to do to get cleared by the program. They told me you're going to have to let the facility feel like you are getting the program, even if you have to fake it. So that is what I did. I faked it.

"They told me to start crying in the group sessions. So, I did that. I'd go to a group session, tell my story and cry. I'm looking around to see if I'm getting any reactions. I could see I'm affecting the counselor. I'd see some of the other patients tearing up.

"So, I'm fitting in. I'm one of the guys. When people come into program, I'm the first to greet them and show them around and everything like that because I'm trying to get out of this place, and I'm trying to please the counselors. Then another player comes in, a player by the name of Lloyd Daniels, who is with the San Antonio Spurs. They call him Sweet Pea. I became like a big brother to him. I taught Sweet Pea the rules of the place. We worked out together. To this day, I still talk to Sweet Pea.

"I'm staying in the facility while people are leaving. I am now the oldest guy in the place. Then I decided it's time to get out. I graduated from the treatment program. I got a certificate saying I'm sober from drugs. I called a friend of mine to pick me up from the airport, and he took me back to Oakland.

"The friend has a bunch of joints rolled up, laced with cocaine, rock cocaine. That was the first time I'd ever smoked a laced joint. Just like that. I'm high again. I'm right back to where I started. And that night, we smoked over sixty joints! The monster in me is awakened, and that happened on the ride straight from the airport. The team was expecting to see a new Chris. What they saw was exactly the same Chris who had gone off to rehab.

"And I wasn't fooling anyone. Everybody knew, the coaches, the players, that I was back to getting high. They could tell just from my appearance."

The media was pressing the Warriors, wanting to know if they knew Washburn was involved with drugs. Warriors' management danced around the question. Finnane revealed that management never asked Washburn directly if he was using drugs and that they never tested him for drugs. But he conceded that the team had been tipped off about Washburn's drug use. Finnane told the *San Francisco Chronicle* that the team had received reports from time to time that Washburn was using drugs and that they had followed up and investigated the reports, but he claimed, "We couldn't pin anything down."

With Washburn entering the drug treatment program, the media began to investigate the timeline for Washburn's drug use. When interviewed, North Carolina State University basketball coach Jim Valvano said that to the best of his knowledge, Washburn did not have a problem with drugs while at NC State and that he had entered the university's voluntary drug-testing program while there.

CHRIS WASHBURN: "Len Bias turned me on to crack in my dorm room, but it's true that coach Valvano or his basketball program knew nothing about it."

When Washburn entered the drug treatment program, Washburn's agent, Larry Gillman, met with Warriors management and revised Washburn's contract, changing it from four years guaranteed to two years guaranteed. Under the terms of the modified contract, Washburn would have to make the club the final two years of the contract to be paid.

The NBA Players Association filed a grievance on Washburn's behalf, claiming that the Warriors could not penalize a player for volunteering to submit to treatment.

The case was argued in New York before a Professor Dean Collins, who arbitrated grievances for the NBA. In August 1987, Collins ruled that both Washburn's contract and the revision of his contract violated the Players Association's contract with the NBA.

Washburn returned from rehab in time for the Warriors push for the playoffs. During the final three weeks of the season, he was used sparingly except in blowout games. He played eight games after his return from rehab but was only on the court for no more than fifteen minutes in four of them. In the final game of the year, Washburn scored seventeen points, powering the Warriors to a win. In clutch time, in the fourth quarter, he scored ten points. He hit eight of thirteen shots from the floor and grabbed five rebounds. It looked like Washburn had never left for rehab.

Golden State managed to make the playoffs, improving by ten games over the previous year. The Warriors finished 42-40 for third place in the Pacific conference and fifth in the Western Conference. In one year of coaching, Karl had brought the Warriors from the bottom seven to the top eight teams in the league.

Washburn returned to the Warriors in late March. He had gained twenty-five pounds in rehab, and it would take time before he was back in shape to play. The Warriors let it be known that whether Washburn played would depend on coach Karl. Karl, in turn, said he would make Washburn's conditioning and attitude the two criteria for judging Washburn's readiness to return.

Finnane allowed Washburn to talk briefly about his drug treatment experience with the press. Then he said the subject would be off limits to reporters because "We're running a basketball team, not a drug rehab center." Washburn told the press, "I've weighed the negatives and positives about my life. I've led the life of a dope addict, and I don't want to go back."

On March 29, 1987, Washburn stood up at the Warriors bench, took off his sweat suit and walked to the scorer's table to check into the game. Warm applause rippled through the arena as Washburn entered the game with seventeen seconds left in the half. The applause grew louder as Washburn smiled and looked out at the crowd.

CHRIS WASHBURN: "It was a real surprise, the fan reaction to my reappearance. I had let the team down when I had gone to rehab, but they were welcoming me back."

Washburn only played three more minutes in the third and fourth quarters. He had one rebound and missed his only shot. It was too early to tell whether he would be an asset to the team.

On April 2, Washburn got his first extensive playing time since returning to the team, and his performance was a disaster. Washburn, still ten pounds overweight, shot 3-for-ten and had four rebounds in twenty-one minutes. Two of his jump shots were blocked. A *San Francisco Chronicle* reporter noted that it was "…maddening to see Washburn often wandering six feet or more from the basket while other players crashed the boards with authority" and concluded that the "lack of efficiency is understandable, but not the lack of effort."

The Warriors made their first playoff appearance since 1977. It was an impressive achievement for coach Karl. Frustrated, Karl had threatened to shake up the team with trades, but management had persuaded Karl not to make changes for the sake of change, and that strategy now appeared to be paying off. There was talk of Karl contending for the NBA Coach of the Year title.

In the opening round, the Warriors, seeded fifth in the Western Conference, played the Utah Jazz. In the second game, the Warriors rallied from a thirty-one-point deficit to take a brief lead late in the fourth quarter, but they fell behind 103-100 with seven seconds to go.

The Warriors were unable to get the tying three-pointer before time elapsed. The Warriors' Greg Ballard tried to foul Karl Malone before time expired but could not get the call.

Ballard had Malone in a virtual headlock in trying to get the foul. Then Ballard pushed Malone away as time expired. Malone flipped the ball at Ballard, but Ballard threw it back.

All hell broke loose. The benches emptied. In the middle of the brawl was Chris Washburn, who got into it with several Jazz players and had to be wrestled to the floor by teammate Joe Barry Carroll.

CHRIS WASHBURN: "I wasn't playing that much, and I'm at odds with the team a little bit. At the end of the game, a commotion happened on the floor. I couldn't really see because I was on the bench. Then I saw a lot of pushing and shoving, and I saw a chance to get in good with the team, let them see that I'm standing up for them. So, I ran out and jumped into the middle of the brawl and threw the first punch. I hit the closest guy, Carey Scurry, a forward for Utah Jazz. Then I went to find somebody else, and I swung at Mark Eaton.

"Then I tried to get to Karl Malone, who was being escorted off the court. I was trying to find somebody to fight with, anybody, but my teammates grabbed me and took me to the locker room. I was confined to my hotel room for my own safety. I had security outside my door. I think the team appreciated what I did, although it probably wasn't too smart on my part. They could see I was a team player, ready to stand up for my teammates."

The Warriors surprisingly prevailed, upsetting the Jazz and winning three straight games and the series three games to two. In the second round, the Warriors lost to the powerful Los Angeles Lakers, four games to one. The Lakers went on to win the championship, beating the Boston Celtic four games to two.

In the playoffs, Washburn only appeared in one game against the Jazz and four games against the Lakers. Three of those games were double-digit losses. Washburn averaged 2.2 points and two rebounds, playing six minutes per game.

The Warriors' 1986-87 year had been successful, but Washburn's first year had been a major bust. When Washburn had voluntarily entered the drug rehabilitation center in Van Nuys the previous January, the Warriors met with Larry Gillman and revised the contract, changing it from four years guaranteed to two years guaranteed. Under the revised contract, Washburn would have to make the club in the final two years of the contract to be paid.

Gillman filed another grievance, charging that the contract change violated the Association's contract with the league. One cannot penalize a player for voluntarily submitting to treatment. The case went to arbitration, and Washburn won. Both the clause in Washburn's contract and the revision of the contract violated the Players Association agreement with the league, the arbitrator ruled.

With the season over, the Warriors were looking ahead to next year. Washburn's rookie season was one that the Warriors would have liked to forget. Washburn, however, was hardly alone.

There were various drug-related problems that plagued players from the 1986 NBA draft. Most notable had been the death of highly touted University of Maryland superstar Len Bias. Bias died less than two days after being selected second overall by the defending champion Boston Celtics. His death was ruled an overdose that resulted from taking the drug cocaine.[6]

Other problems involving drugs hampered the careers of Roy Tarpley, the number seven pick, and William Bedford, number six. A power forward and center in the NBA, Tarpley's career started off well, as he won the NBA Sixth Man of the Year Award in 1988. It was eventually derailed, however, in 1995, when he was permanently banned by the NBA due to his drug and alcohol abuse. Tarpley died on January 9, 2015, at age fifty.

Chuck Person, the number four draft pick, was selected Rookie of the Year, but he was arrested in 2017 while assistant head coach for Auburn, charged with taking bribes for steering players to certain financial managers.

William Bedford, the sixth man taken in the 1986 draft, played for the Suns, Detroit Pistons, and the San Antonio Spurs in six NBA seasons. Projected as a can't miss star, Bedford's NBA career was marred by drug use, and he missed the 1988-89 NBA season as a result. Bedford's drug problems continued after he stopped playing in the NBA, and he ended up in prison. Such failures have caused some observers to call the 1986 NBA draft the worst of all time.

Not all draft picks turned out to be disaster stories. North Carolina center Brad Daugherty, the top overall selection in the 1986 NBA draft, had a solid career.' He reached five All-Star games in his career. His 19.0 ppg leads all players drafted in the 1986 draft, and he had his Cavaliers contending in the Central Division and Eastern Conference. Back issues would limit his career to just eight seasons.

---

6. "1986 NBA Draft," Wikipedia, January 28, 2025, https://en.wikipedia.org/wiki/1986_NBA_draft.

Remarkably, despite his problems with drugs and adjusting to the pros, Washburn still figured in the Warriors' future plans. When asked about Washburn, Karl said he thought the kid could play. "A lot depends on Chris Washburn," Karl said. "He has to improve the mental aspect of his game, but I'm still excited about him."

Karl was encouraged by the fact that Washburn seemed to work harder after returning from drug rehabilitation. He was scheduled to attend Pete Newell's big man camp, summer league ball with the Warriors, and then head to the Warriors training camp.

Given their experience with Washburn so far, the Warriors were cautious in expressing their opinion about whether Washburn could turn his career around. Warriors' management insisted in interviews with the press that Washburn had improved.

He did well in summer camp. In the last game of the camp, Washburn scored twenty-three points in the Warriors 129-118 loss. He had worked as hard as many of the free-agent long shots who didn't have the luxury of a guaranteed contract as Washburn did. The Warriors kept him in the Bay Area much of the summer, and he played in as many summer league games as possible.

In June, for three days a week, Washburn was given individual instruction by a Golden State coach. He never missed a workout, and he even called the coach if he was going to be a little bit late. He was also placed on a weight and nutrition program and increased his bench press from 190 to 255 pounds. He improved his speed and endurance and learned a little about rebounding.

Golden State's management agreed that the 6'11 Washburn would have to be more assertive on the boards the upcoming season. Among all the mismatches of the Lakers series in the NBA finals, none was more damaging than the rebounding: L.A. averaged 48.4 per game to Golden State's 37.8. And since Larry Smith averaged 15.6 rebounds per game against Los Angeles—41.3 percent of his team's total—the need for help was all the more obvious.

In Warriors training camp in October, Washburn continued to impress. He had entered the training camp weighing 280 pounds but was now down to 242 pounds. The conditioning program appeared to be paying off, as he impressed with his improved physical prowess.

Management, however, still worried about his mental readjustment. "He has normal breakdowns for a young player—his execution and his ability to read the situations," Karl told the San Jose *Mercury News* newspaper.

Warriors' management did not know—or more likely did not want to know—that Washburn was still struggling with a drug problem. Every chance he had, Washburn would be in projects looking to get high. Washburn was struggling with his drug problem.

CHRIS WASHBURN: "I was mad that I wasn't able to do all the things on the basketball court that I knew I could do because of my drug habit. I always wanted to change, but I wanted to make a change the way I wanted to. The truth is I wanted to do the drugs when I wanted to. And because of that, I didn't see any reason to quit. The truth was I liked smoking cocaine. It gave me a chance to escape. It gave me a chance to get out of depression. The problem was when I came down, all my problems were still there."

As the 1987-88 season opened, the Los Angeles Lakers were predicted to be a lock to win the Western conference and the NBA championship. Second place in the Western Conference was expected to be a fight between Golden

State, Portland, and Seattle. The Warriors were expecting Washburn to contribute significantly to their title run.

"Players around the league are gonna see a different person in me," Washburn predicted in one press interview.

In mid-November, Washburn was expected to play center for Joe Barry Carroll, who was out of the lineup with a sore right foot, but he injured his right thigh during practice. Don Nelson, the Warriors executive vice president, blows up at Washburn and throws him out of a shootaround. Nelson snapped at Washburn: "You're doggin' it, get out of here." Washburn was summoned to Nelson's office and chewed out.

It was a sign that the Warriors were about to give up on their prize 1986 number one pick. Karl fueled the rumors by saying the Warriors were willing to listen to overtures from any club that may want to pursue Washburn. He added that he expected Washburn to be with the Warriors at the end of the season, admitting no team has made an offer. Any team wanting Washburn would have to factor Washburn's high salary into the team's salary cap.

Washburn became disenchanted. Despite his continued drug use, he thought he had worked hard on his game and had improved. But he had played in only eight of the Warriors' first 18 games of the 1987-88 season.

CHRIS WASHBURN: "I was disappointed. I thought I had worked hard over the summer, but all it got me was sitting deeper on the bench. I thought I should be playing more minutes."

The *New York Post* reported that one team was going to make a play for Washburn but did not name the team. A prominent rumor had Washburn going to the Sacramento Kings for center LaSalle Thompson in a three-way deal involving the Nets' Orlando Woolridge and Kelly Tripucka-But nothing seemed to work out. Then Chris Washburn got a call from Don Nelson.

CHRIS WASHBURN: "Don Nelson called me, Coach Karl and my agent, Larry Gillman, into his office. I didn't really know Don Nelson at that time. He was new to me. Like I said, I'm not a big basketball fan. I don't really watch the NBA on TV. So, I didn't know anything about his playing days or anything like that. When he called me in, he told me that I was a bum. He said that I was not doing my job on the court. He told me that they wanted to buy out my contract.

"I'm just sitting there, quiet, taking it all in. My agent is doing the talking, and I'm listening to how they're trying to get rid of me. Nelson says that the team can't find anybody who wants me, 'but we're trying to get rid of you.' I heard enough and left the room. They spoke a little more after I left.

"It wasn't much longer after that that I got a call about three in the morning from coach Karl. He told me that I needed to get my ass up and to pack my bags. I've been traded to Atlanta. Don't miss your flight. I think I could've declined the trade, but I said, 'Okay. No problem.'"

Washburn had been traded to the Atlanta Hawks for the rights for forward Ken Barlow. Nelson acknowledged that the Warriors had been trying to move Washburn for some time. It had nothing to do with drugs, but more with character, Nelson claimed.

Barlow was not even in the NBA. He was playing in Israel. He would never play in the NBA. In essence, the Warriors received nothing for Washburn. By trading him, the Warriors had admitted their big mistake. The Warriors had given up on Chris Washburn.

Photos

Washburn at play in the NBA

Washburn talking about his amazing life

Washburn, Chepesiuk at contract signing for book

Washburn with the Warriors

Dunking the ball. Washburn was compared to Shaq O'Neal

Chris Washburn being guarded by Curt Rambis

Chris Washburn at the restaurant he owned in Hickory

*Washburn at draft holding Golden State
shirt who drafted him third.*

Washburn Profile

7

ATLANTA BOUND

"Sometimes, I would find somebody with a house, somebody I felt comfortable with. I'd go there, park my Porsche in front, go into the house and stay most of the night smoking crack. Most of my life focused on finding my next high. I had turned into a rich junkie." ~ Chris Washburn

Overnight, Chris Washburn was traded to Atlanta. He felt it was coming, but he was still stunned by the deal. He was not happy at how the Warriors had treated him. He had worked hard during the summer to get in shape and get his game back, but when it came time to play, all the Warriors did was keep him on the bench. He had played in only eight of the Warriors' eighteen games so far in the 1986-87 season.

Don Nelson, the Warriors' general manager, told Washburn that they had been shopping him around the league, but nobody would take him. Washburn had not been reading the newspapers. Although he knew the Warriors were dissatisfied with his play, he had no clue that the team was planning to trade him.

CHRIS WASHBURN: "When I thought about it, I liked the idea of going to Atlanta. It would give me a fresh start. I think I really had outstayed my welcome in California. I wasn't hanging with any members of the team because my circle at the time was a drug circle. Golden State really didn't have any big names. I was excited about going and taking my talent to another team with talent. But the problem about me going to Atlanta was that I was bringing myself and my drug problem with me."

Cliff Levingston, a Hawks power forward from 1984 to 1990, who played with Washburn, was happy to see Washburn traded to the Hawks.

CLIFF LEVINGSTON "I thought it was gonna be a good trade. We need another big guy, and he was a big body who could cover the middle."

So, as Washburn left Oakland, Washburn was upbeat about the trade. He told the *Atlanta-Journal Constitution*, "I've got to prove myself. I do. Everywhere people have doubt. But as long as the team has enthusiasm for me, everything will be alright. We'll work it out."

Washburn had rejected the Warriors' offer to buy out his contract, but he did agree to re-structure his contract with Atlanta and take a pay cut so Atlanta could stay under the salary cap. Washburn's four-year contract with Golden State was reported to be $675,000. The Hawks did not make public the terms of his Atlanta contract, but published reports said he was receiving $375,000 for the 1987-88 season to fit under the team's salary cap and would receive the rest of the money from his original contract over the next three seasons.

As soon as he arrived in Atlanta, even before he checked into his hotel or met with his team, Washburn headed for the projects to find some crack to get high.

CHRIS WASHBURN: "My first day in Atlanta I was up the entire night getting high with a friend of mine who had picked me up from the airport. The next day, I went to the press conference. I was coming down from the high. I got a warm reception, but nobody at the press conference knew anything about my condition."

Washburn was described at the press conference as "happy but dazed." In speaking to reporters, Washburn said, "Things there (Golden State) were not the way I wanted them, but I got no bad things to say about coach (Karl)."

In speaking with reporters, Tree Rollins, the Atlanta Hawks captain, revealed that the Hawks would not have made the trade for Washburn without the approval of the Hawk team. Rollins, who would be responsible for showing Washburn the ropes, told the *Atlanta Journal-Constitution*, "Remember, this is a veteran team that's been together for a while. We're strong among ourselves. We won't allow anybody to come in here and disrupt our chemistry. I think Chris will be okay but if he's not…Look we got one guy off the team (Eddie Johnson, Rollins' cousin) because of drugs. We don't want another mistake. I believe we can get Chris in our family atmosphere and bring him along."

After Washburn's arrival in Atlanta, he met a young woman we will identify as Jessie R. at a basketball game against the Chicago Bulls. Jessie had come for an autograph from Michael Jordan when Chris spotted her in the crowd and asked her name. Washburn invited Jessie out to dinner. The two became a couple, and Jessie moved in with Chris.

JESSIE R: "It's hard not to like Chris. I look at him as a big teddy bear. He is very likable and very charismatic. He's just a lot of fun. I know the girls liked him. He had a lot them. He would be gone from the house for long stretches.

Washburn says Jessie misread his stretches of time from home, and he doesn't look upon himself as a womanizer.

CHRIS WASHBURN: "I had my shot at groupie girls. They would be around in the different cities in which we played. They were at the airport and the hotels. They would be at different clubs I went to. They knew when I was coming to town. But that didn't really affect me because my whole thing was trying to find drugs. When I did find them, I would look for a place where I could smoke. I wasn't thinking about the girls. I'm thinking about the drugs. I can see how it would look like I was messing around because I would go out in the evening and not come back until the morning."

The Hawks knew that Washburn had a drug problem while playing for Golden State, and the team claimed to have him drug tested, but Washburn said this did not happen.

CHRIS WASHBURN: "They never really drug tested me. The only time I was actually drug tested was at the rehab center. They left me on my own. What they did was give me a therapist to talk to. When our appointment came up, I would come in and go to sleep. He'd wake me up and say, 'okay, your time is up.' I would get up and leave. We didn't talk about anything because I was sleeping. I had been up all-night smoking crack and was starting to come down, so I went to sleep the entire hour. It really didn't matter to the therapist, I guess, because he was still getting paid."

Whereas Golden State's coach George Karl was in his first year when Washburn played for him, Atlanta coach Mike Fratello was garnering a reputation as one of the best coaches in the NBA despite not playing in the league. "Fratello was an assistant coach at Villanova under Rollie Massimino before going to the NBA as an assistant coach for the Atlanta Hawks." During Hubie Brown's tenure, "Fratello was named Coach of the Year for the 1985–86

NBA season. His teams would go on to qualify for the playoffs in eleven of his 16 seasons as a head coach."[7] Fratello's coaching of Washburn, however, was different than that of George Karl's.

CHRIS WASHBURN: "Playing under Fratello was better for me because he wasn't doing all of the after-practice stuff Karl had me do. Karl would work me extra after practice. and all I wanted to do was leave practice as soon as possible and go and get high."

Coach Fratello was planning to bring Washburn along slowly, but because of an injury to Kevin Willis, Washburn was thrust into play in his first game against Utah. Washburn scored two points and hauled in five rebounds. In the next game against the Houston Rockets, Washburn played 19 minutes and finished with eight points and five rebounds.

The Hawks were optimistic about Washburn's performance. Fratello said they would give Washburn time and that he "had much to catch up on."

But by Washburn's own admission, he was a drug user first and a basketball player second, and he spent most of his time when not practicing or playing basketball in the projects getting high. Washburn had come to Atlanta accompanied by fellow drug user, Uncle Ted Hodge, who knew Atlanta well and the places where he could get crack. Hodge would go into the ghetto, driving his nephew's conspicuous Porsche, and people would think it was Chris Washburn, not his uncle, buying crack.

Despite the positive rhetoric about Washburn and his encouraging play, Fratello was reluctant to use Washburn in close games. In a game on December 30, Kevin Willis,

---

7. "Mike Fratello," Wikipedia, March 13, 2025, https://en.wikipedia.org/wiki/Mike_Fratello.

Tree Rollins, and Jon Koncak were in early foul trouble, and Antoine Carr was out in the third quarter with a hyperextended knee, but instead of using Washburn, Fratello turned to seldom-used Scott Hastings as the big man in the middle. Hastings played thirteen minutes and had nine points and four rebounds.

CHRIS WASHBURN: "I really didn't care about whether I played or not. I just wanted the game to be over. I wanted the practice to be over, whatever, so I could go out and get high. I wasn't even paying attention to what was happening on the court, really."

Almost every day, Washburn would head for the projects looking for crack. He lived about an hour away from the arena where he practiced and played, but he began dating a woman who lived close to the arena. Washburn would be out most of the night doing crack, then often return to the girl's apartment, clean himself up, and head for a practice or a game.

CHRIS WASHBURN: "After a game or practice, the players would often all get together and head for a fast-food restaurant, like a Burger King, to get something to eat. After that, we'd all split up, I didn't go home. I headed for the projects. By now it was late at night. Back then in Atlanta, I found a place right behind the arena, the Omni. It is called Vine City. It was one of the big drug areas.

"I'd go there and find some young boys, drug pushers. I could tell they were pushers by the way they were acting. I would set things up. I'd tell them I'll be back later that night after the game. I would return and stay all night, smoking crack.

"Sometimes, I would find somebody with a house, somebody I felt comfortable with. I'd go there, park my Porsche in front, go into the house and stay most of the night smoking crack. Most of my life focused on finding my next high. I had turned into a rich junkie.

"The dudes with whom I was doing crack knew who I was, but I wasn't worried about whether they'd tell on me. They didn't run in my circle. Besides, I had the money. I was turning them on for nothing. It didn't cost them a cent. If anything happened to me, they couldn't get high for free."

"Yeah, I knew it was risky. I was in the projects, a tough area, but the thought of danger didn't dawn on me at the time. I hired a couple of home boys as security. They ended up being my drug runners. They'd go out, find crack and bring it back to me. Sometimes, I'd give them money and they wouldn't come back. They'd smoke the crack themselves. But I would always find the crack and my drug habit got worse. I eventually had to pawn my jewelry. When I had the money, I'd go back to get my jewelry, but the pawn shop would double the price on me. They would screw me. So how much was I spending on crack? At one time, about $1200 to $1500 a day."

What about when Washburn was on the road? How did he get his drugs then?

CHRIS WASHBURN: "As my habit got a little more addictive, I would bring drugs with me on the road. But there were times when I didn't bring them with me, and the urge would hit me. So, I would get a cab and tell the cabbie to take me to the projects, and he'd take me there. I'd tell him to come back at a certain time and get me. I was very trusting, naïve, because I was going to places that where dangerous, and I wasn't familiar with. I could have found some bad trouble."

Washburn never had to deal with violence, but that does not mean that Washburn didn't see it happen.

CHRIS WASHBURN: "I was driving my big Mercedes, and I ended up at a place where I could buy crack. Somebody else was there, and he said we can go to a house which had a basement where we could smoke with more privacy. So, I went to the house with him. The basement was under the house and had a dirt floor where I sat.

"I had about $600 worth of drugs on me. There were two other people there smoking as well. So, while we're down there smoking, two other guys came inside and stood in front of the other two people that were there before me and sitting on the ground. One of the guys that came suddenly punched one of the sitting guys in the face. His partner got behind him and put him in a choke hold and choked him out.

"While the sitting guy was out cold, they checked his pockets and took his drugs and money. I'm just sitting there, smoking. It's like I'm watching a show on TV. It had no effect on me. The two guys who choked the man out then looked at me. They turned around and left. They could easily have jumped me as well, I had way more drugs than the choked-out guy had on him, and I had way more money on me.

"We thought the choked-out guy was dead, but he comes to and shakes his head. I asked him if he wanted a hit. He nodded yes, so I gave him a hit of crack. I felt sorry for the guy. What happened to him could have happened to me. And it did…later."

The Hawks were not oblivious to Washburn's crack lifestyle as he descended deeper into the black hole of drug addiction. The Atlanta police knew that Washburn was hustling his next fix in the projects.

CLIFF LEVINGSTON: "The police were coming to me and Tree Rollins and telling us, 'We're gonna raid a drug house. Can you tell Chris Washburn not to be there?' We'd go to

Chris. He is like 'Man, I'm not over there.' I'd say, 'Come on, Chris. Just don't go over there.' Then a couple of days later, the cops would tell us, 'Look, you gotta tell your boy to stay away from the hood. We're getting ready to raid it.' So, we go to Chris again, and tell him: 'Chris, they're telling us you're over there. Stop.' He'd say: 'I wasn't over there.' I'd say, 'Chris, you were in your car.' Chris thought no one really knew, but we all knew. We just never talked about it."

Levingston didn't know if his young teammate would gain control of his drug habit.

LEVINGSTON: "We talked among ourselves about who's gonna keep an eye on Chris when we go on the road? Who's gonna keep a check on him in Atlanta? It was a team effort thing because we knew he needed help. But I didn't think his will was strong enough to fight the drugs off. You're a young kid with a lot of money at your disposal, and you got ways of basically having people do things for you and covering for you. So, I didn't know if he was gonna be strong enough to recover."

Meanwhile, Washburn's drug addiction got so bad that he would smoke crack on an airplane.

CHRIS WASHBURN: "Sometimes we would take a flight, and I would go into the bathroom and do crack. It might be a two-hour flight, and I would be in the bathroom for the whole two hours. I would unplug the smoke detector. I would sit down on the toilet and smoke, and every time I exhaled, I would just push that sink thing down and the air would suck out.

"I would come out of the bathroom, sweating, after an hour or so. I would hear the intercom, and the flight stewardess saying, 'We're about to land.' My teammates would look at me and see me sweating. They'd laugh because they knew

I'm high. The coaches probably knew, too, but they didn't sit with us."

By the end of 1988, Washburn had played only four games since joining the team on December 16. In his best game he scored eight points and five rebounds in a victory over the Houston Rockets.

Still, the Hawks claimed that they were impressed with Washburn's limited play. In an interview with the *Chicago Sun-Times,* Hawks assistant coach Brian Hill enthused: "He is still a little green and has some growing up to do, but our guys love him. He's been here every day, busted his tail every practice. He's been wonderful. We're thinking that he's someone who just got caught up in the system."

Everybody seemed to want to protect Chris Washburn. In a lengthy interview with the *Charlotte Observer,* Uncle Ted Hodge claimed Washburn had three drug tests per week and had made mandatory attendance at four counseling sessions per week when the Hawks are in Atlanta, or at least one in each city when they are on the road.

Washburn also had a 1 am curfew. Hodge told the newspaper: "He can go out and find that someone is using cocaine. He's gotten out of there right away."

Today, Washburn says that Uncle Ted's comments in that article represent a series of half-truths.

CHRIS WASHBURN: "It looked like we were abiding by the rules, but I had no problem getting access to drugs. A lot of times my uncle would provide them for me. The whole system was based on the honor system where you would bring the urine samples to them. They would give me a cup, and I would go into the bathroom, take my urine sample, and come back out. No one was standing beside me when I took the sample. But it wasn't my urine sample. My uncle would bring in a sample he collected from some dude and pass it off to me. I would give him my sample and I'd give the sample my uncle gave me to the facility."

Jessie R. didn't get along with Washburn's mother or uncle, and she thought Uncle Ted did not have Chris's best interests at heart.

JESSIE R: "Ted was really two faced and slick. He was helping to feed Chris's drug habit, and I know he was using Chris's money for his own purposes."

As for the mother, Savannah, she confronted Jessie, accusing her of being a gold digger.

JESSIE R: "Chris's mom wrote me a letter that said, something about how I wanted him for his money, and I wasn't gonna get it. I wrote her back, telling her I wasn't doing that. I was trying to help him. I'm not one of those people you're talking about. I'm in the military. I got a good career and my own money. I was pissed."

Early in his career, Washburn had signed over power of attorney to his first agent, who had stolen $600,000 from his Golden State contract money. His second agent saw the extent of Washburn's drug and money problems and suggested Washburn sign over power of attorney to his mother so he wouldn't blow his fortune. Washburn agreed, and his mother took over control of his finances.

By late February, Washburn was still making only cameo appearances for the Hawks. Team management was assuring the public: be patient. Washburn was an investment for the long term. As the *Atlanta Journal-Constitution* put it: "No need to burden him (Chris Washburn) with more responsibility than he's capable of handling."

Washburn's drug addiction, however, just got worse. On March 10, Washburn suffered his worst performance as a Hawk. Fratello inserted Washburn into the game at the 3:48 mark of the first quarter and pulled him from the game at the 1:30 mark. Washburn looked confused and out of position.

SPUD WEBB: "We could see Chris was falling apart. He looked terrible when he came to the arena. Always late. Sometimes we'd have to go to his house and try and find him."

The Hawks were hurting. Tree Rollins and Jon Koncak were injured, and the team needed Washburn to fill in. The Hawks assigned assistant coach Don Chaney, a 6'5" former NBA guard, to work with Washburn. Chaney would work with Washburn over the next four weeks before the playoffs. The objective: accelerate Washburn's "progress."

When Washburn was inserted into a game against the Bucks, coach Fratello noticed one thing. Washburn had entered the game with his shoelaces untied. Washburn lasted 89 seconds before Fratello pulled him.

CHRIS WASHBURN: "Coach would put me in the game when it was almost over. Sometimes they would put me in in the last two minutes of a game. I had sat the whole game. I had a girlfriend come to the game, and I wanted to play. So, I needed to play. But it didn't look like I would, so I untied my shoelaces before the game was over. And then they called me in, I looked down and saw that my shoelaces were untied. I wasn't prepared to get into the game."

On April 15, the Hawks announced that the team would visit the Soviet Union and engage Soviet teams from July 19 to 31. The Hawks would be the first NBA team to play in the Soviet Union. However, only five of the twelve members of the Hawks said they would accept the invitation. Under league rules, the Hawks could require players to agree to participate.

Chris Washburn made headlines by announcing adamantly that he was not going to the Soviet Union and that he would spend his time in North Carolina at home with his family.

JESSIE R: "Chris made me get my passport, and we were ready up until the time we were to leave. Then he said: 'I'm not going.' And we didn't go. I had packed and taken my vacation time from the military to go. I was pissed."

On May 1, Washburn showed up twenty minutes late for a Hawks game, and that made the news. When he arrived at the Omni for the game, he found a sign taped to his locker-room door with the simple message: "Wash, you're late." Washburn said he had asked his uncle to wake him up, but he didn't get it.

By now, the Hawks were losing their patience with Washburn. He had stopped practicing because of a bruised cartilage in his upper left rib cage. But that wasn't good enough for teammate superstar Dominique Wilkins, who chastised Washburn, "First you said it was your heart. Now it's your ribs. Come on, Chris, go to work."

Washburn grabbed his left side in the upper chest area and said, "It's up in there."

Wilkins would have none of it. "I've got fluid in my elbow. My ankle hurts, but I'm practicing."

"You're getting $1.5 million," Washburn snapped.

"I'm an all-star. I'm an all-star because I work hard," Wilkins shot back.

"You know you're going to play. too," Washburn replied.

CHRIS WASHBURN: "I don't hold that against Dominique. He was trying to make the team better. Again, I was a number three pick in the NBA draft, meaning he was expecting me to play the game at a high level. But the truth is: I wasn't holding my end up."

Clearly, frustration was growing with the Hawks over Washburn's team effort. Then in June, Washburn was in Oakland when he was arrested along with a friend for carrying a gun, specifically a five-shot Rosi pistol. Washburn and his pal spent the night in jail.

CHRIS WASHBURN: "After my first season with Atlanta, I returned to Oakland to get some of some stuff out of the house I still owned there. I just bought a Porsche, so me and my girlfriend at the time drove back across country to Oakland. It took us three days. I was smoking cocaine, so I don't remember much of the trip.

"When we got to Oakland, I dropped my girlfriend at my place and went to a friend's apartment, where I wanted to smoke some more dope."

The friend, Derrick Turner, lived in the Adams Point district of Oakland. The hood was a dangerous area known for drug dealing and drive-by shootings.

CHRIS WASHBURN: "I had a gun in the glove compartment of my Porsche. I took it out and tucked it in my pants. But at that time, two police officers were coming around the corners, and they thought they heard shots. What they heard were actually firecrackers. I heard them as well.

"The police stopped at my car, got out of the cruiser, and asked me what was going on. I said I didn't know. They asked if they could search me. I said sure. I had no problem with that. I had forgotten about the gun on me. They found it and arrested me."

Washburn was arrested for possession of a dangerous weapon. A court date was set for the remaining charges of possession of a concealed firearm and possession of a loaded firearm. One of the arresting officers told the press, "We asked him (Chris Washburn) if he had a gun, and he said he did and pointed toward his coat."

The case was complicated by the probation Washburn was still serving for the burglary conviction in Raleigh in 1985. Washburn was in the third year of a five-year probation sentence, part of his plea to a charge of stealing a stereo, which he pled guilty of during his freshman year at North Carolina State University.

Washburn spent the night in an Oakland city jail. The Atlanta Hawks management had little to say about Washburn's arrest outside of indicating he might have violated his after-care program. Team president Stan Kasten said the team would review the entire situation.

On June 7, a felony charge of possession of a dangerous weapon against Washburn was dropped. However, he still faced two weapon-possession misdemeanor charges. On June 10, Washburn was fined $300 and sentenced to eighteen months of probation after he pled no contest to a misdemeanor charge of possession of a concealed weapon. A second misdemeanor charge of possession of a loaded firearm was dropped.

CHRIS WASHBURN: "I was lucky the gun had not been fired. Otherwise, I would have had to go to court, and I would have been in trouble."

The following day, coach Fratello said he wanted to talk with Washburn about the incident before deciding on any team discipline. He was concerned about Washburn as an individual and a Hawks athlete, Fratello explained.

CHRIS WASHBURN: "Coach may have talked to me. I can't remember. But nothing changed. I was still on the team.'"

In August, the team embarked on a groundbreaking three-game tour of the Soviet Union that did not go particularly well. The Hawks players complained about the food, living conditions, and recreation time. Spud Webb, echoing his teammates, complained, "Aw, it was a lot different than I expected. I tell you. I didn't like it. I'll never go back. You're not supposed to say never, but they couldn't pay me all the money in the world to go back there."

Washburn did not accompany the team on the trip. Team doctors wanted him to take time away from basketball and get his life in order. But when the trip was announced in May 1989, Washburn had made his strong feelings about the trip known. He said bluntly, "I ain't going to no Russia."

CHRIS WASHBURN: 'I said no way am I going to Russia. I wanted to go to Hickory and spend time with my family. I was like one of those guys who, if everybody was excited about going to do something, he would be the one guy who said 'no' and go against the grain. I knew nothing about Russia, so I ended up not going,"

Washburn had been a big bust for the Hawks since his trade from Golden State. He had played a mere 174 minutes in 29 games, averaging a paltry two points a game. He was benched in the playoffs and had problems with several Hawks players, including Dominique Wilkins, the team's best player.

In September, Washburn was told to return to the NBA's chosen rehabilitation center in Van Nuys, California. The team suspected that Washburn had had a relapse. Washburn denied that he had one, and his uncle Ted Hodge insisted he had passed the drug tests. He had been working out and even running five miles a day, Uncle Ted claimed.

CHRIS WASHBURN: "The Hawks had become suspicious. There were reports of me in the projects possibly hanging out with drug dealers. I was being drug tested three times, but it was on an honorary system. I would bring in urine to the trainer's office, but it was not mine. My uncle Ted had helped me switch the urine. The team wanted me to come into the Hawks office to be tested right there under supervision.'"

Washburn did that, and he failed a couple of drug tests. He was suspended from the league without pay until doctors cleared him to return to basketball.

Gary Bettman, NBA counsel, said Washburn had received a second strike under the league's substance abuse program. 'Washburn's suspension put the Hawks in a bind. The team could replace Washburn with a minimum-salary player, but Washburn's $777,000 contract would continue to count against the club's salary.'

CHRIS WASHBURN: "At that time, the league was holding on to my money. They were only paying me enough to cover my bills, plus a little spending money, but not my salary."

In late December, the Hawks announced publicly that Washburn, who was completing his eighty-five days of rehab, was making "good progress" toward recovery and that they expected him to be out of the rehab center in a week or two.

Washburn was indeed doing well. He had complied with the requirements of the treatment program.

CHRIS WASHBURN: "I was doing what was needed, what was asked of me. I wasn't doing any drugs. I was following the program, going to the meetings, helping new patients when they came in. I was showing compassion for others, things like that. But the facility was leery of me. It knew I could easily relapse. They watched me closely. They would check my visitation list to see who I was seeing."

Washburn was given a clean bill of health and released from the rehabilitation center in Van Nuys. He would have a couple of weeks outpatient care before being allowed to practice with the Hawks. Washburn spent two weeks at his mother's home. He was no longer receiving his $400,000 salary, although his treatment was paid for by the Hawks. Another relapse, and he would have to forfeit his contract with the Hawks and would be banned from the NBA for at least two years.

Meanwhile, Peter Golenbock released his expose on the North Carolina State University basketball program. It contained a number of shocking allegations, including fixed players' grades, positive drug tests being kept secret, and players receiving money, cars, and other items from a special fund. NC State threatened to sue Golenbock, and the original publisher, Simon and Schuster, withdrew publication. Carroll and Graf stepped up and agreed to publish the book.

Golenbock relied on anonymous sources but declined to release the tapes of the interviews he said he had made with sources. An unidentified source was quoted as saying: "Wash (Washburn) would play games on coke. The first half he'd play great, and then the coke would wear off, and in the second half he wouldn't do anything."

Richard Lauffler, retired head of NC State's physical education department, said in an interview published in the *News and Observer* of Raleigh, North Carolina, that three failing grades on Washburn's transcript were changed to passing grades in 1985. In the article, Lauffler said he took his concerns to the University's president, Chancellor Bruce Poulton. Poulton denied the allegation. Two members of the university's physical education department did not back Lauffler's claim.

CHRIS WASHBURN: "I never read the book, but I heard what the author said about me. They said I missed classes, but as I said earlier, I wasn't in school that first year after I got suspended, so I don't know how my grades could have been changed."

More controversy followed for Washburn. On June 13, Atlanta Hawks president Stan Kasten announced that Washburn had violated the terms of his rehabilitation program and had returned to treatment. Once released from the Van Nuys, California-based facility, Washburn had gone back almost immediately to his old ways.

CHRIS WASHBURN: "When the new Chris left that facility, the old Chris took over. I thought I could be sneaky. I went back to the team, and they could tell I had not changed. I disappointed them. My uncle was continuing to make the drug runs into the projects for me. But it was still the same outcome for me. I was still using drugs."

This time, the Hawks put Washburn in another facility: the Ridgeview Institute in Smyrna, Georgia. Washburn was skating on thin ice. If Washburn failed the drug test a third time, he would be banned from the NBA for life, although he could apply for reinstatement after two years. Washburn hated Ridgeview.

CHRIS WASHBURN: "The team wanted me to go into treatment again because my car had been seen in the project a few times. Ridgeview wasn't like Van Nuys. It was a different place. There was a different therapist, different things. As I told you before, once I get used to something,

I'm used to it. You're not sending me to a place that I'm not accustomed to. I refused to go to Ridgeview.

"I left the treatment center that day and went to a crack house. Later that night, I heard on ESPN that I was banned from the league. I was getting high when I saw it on TV."

The third strike had arrived, and Washburn had struck out. He had forfeited his 1988-89 salary. He was banned from playing in the NBA. The remaining years of his contract were voided.

Washburn told Jessie R. that he had been banned from the NBA.

JESSIE R.: "He called me the day he learned he was banned and being sent to rehab. I had been telling Chris for a long time that he needed to get right. Chris was a big kid caught in a grown body. That's what he was. I think when he was younger, they never let him be a kid. He was always big, and people always treated him as older. He never got to play with cars or trucks. So, what did he do when he got money? He went out and bought cars, played with them, and tore them up. He never had the responsibility of taking care of anything. He didn't worry about the consequences."

The big question: Would Chris Washburn now start worrying about the consequences?

CHRIS WASHBURN: "I was cut off from the money coming in from my contract. Yeah, I thought I had money in the bank. But being young and naive I didn't realize I had lost my job and would have no more money to put in the bank. So, after I was banned, I went to the bank like always and tried to take money out. The ATM said insufficient funds. I went into the bank to find out how much money I really had. It was an awakening. I was running out of money. What was I to do?"

8

BANNED

"So, drugs were dominating my whole life then. I was just obsessed about getting my next high. I would sit on the floor on the edge of my Whirlpool tub in my empty house to smoke the crack. But I didn't care. As long as I could get high." ~ Chris Washburn

On July 27, 1989, Chris Washburn asked the NBA to be readmitted ASAP to the substance abuse clinic in Van Nuys, California, for the third time. The NBA sounded encouraging. "The goal here isn't to punish the players," Gary Bettman, the NBA's general counsel, told the press, "It's to get the players well. As far as Chris goes, we encouraged him to go back to Van Nuys, and we'll pay for all of it. We're not going to throw any of the guys out on the street."

Chris Washburn would never re-enter the rehab program. His tenure in the NBA would be a total bust. *Sports Illustrated* would dub Washburn the second biggest draft bust in NBA history, and Washburn was not yet twenty-four years of age.

Drafted third by the Golden State Warriors in the 1986 draft, Washburn's struggles with substance abuse and rehabilitation did not help. The Warriors unloaded Washburn to the Atlanta Hawks for nothing, a player who never joined the NBA. Washburn failed rehabilitation twice with the Hawks and received the infamous third strike, banning him from the NBA. Consequently, he had forfeited a $1.6 million salary. Yet, despite his problems, money was still available.

CHRIS WASHBURN: "The money from the contract was cut, but I still had access to money from my bank account. I didn't know how much, but it was enough that it lasted another couple of years before I had to start pawning jewelry and things like that."

To add insult to injury, Washburn discovered his agent, Larry Gillman, was stealing from him.

WASHBURN: "Gillman was flying out to California. So was my mother. He flew first class, and he had my mother fly coach. It got my mother to thinking as to how Gillman was handling my money if he had to put her in coach. She contacted Larry, and they agreed to meet in Washington DC, a good point between New York City and my hometown. He was supposed to bring all my tax stuff with him so my mom could review it. But all he brought was a little notepad. He didn't have any records to show my mother.

"We found out that he hadn't been paying my bills like he was supposed to, and that he was spending my money. So, I fired him. I found a new agent, a guy by the name of Bill McCandless, out of Boston. He's now living in Atlanta. He met with me and my mom, looked at my financial records and got my tax situation back in shape."

Washburn's predicament would have been devastating for anyone hooked on drugs and losing a million-plus-dollar career, but he was surprisingly unfazed by his situation.

CHRIS WASHBURN: "I really didn't have deep feelings about the ban and what impact it had on my life because, at that time, I was so heavily into drugs, and the addict's life was my focus. My heavy drug use dulled my perception of what had happened to me. I was still living in a nice house. I was still driving nice cars. I had jewelry. So, the impact wasn't immediate. It hadn't settled in. At the time, I loved doing drugs. When they took basketball away from me, I was okay with it. No more practice in the morning or putting out on the basketball court. I could get as high as I wanted to."

Washburn could not stay out of trouble. On October 10, 1989, Atlanta's Black Cat Drug Enforcement strike force was working undercover. Washburn was with the two drug dealers, and he was arrested and charged with disorderly conduct. Later, he was charged with giving the police a false name.

Sergeant Rodney Rancifer of the strike force told the media, "He (Washburn) didn't have any drugs on him. He didn't have anything. He was flat broke." Washburn spent twenty-four hours in the DeKalb County jail and was released.

CHRIS WASHBURN: "I was just there on a trespassing charge. They gave me a warning and let me go. The fact I was an ex-NBA player might have helped me."

Washburn had another brush with the law later in December when he was arrested on criminal trespassing charges at Techwood Homes, described by police as a drug-infested public housing development.

CHRIS WASHBURN: "I was in Techwood Homes, and there was a shootout going on. I needed a place to hide. I ran into an apartment building that had an upstairs and three floors. I ran to the next floor. There was a police officer there who ran behind me up the flight of stairs. He thought I was involved in the shooting. A woman who was there said I wasn't involved with the shooting. It wasn't me. I received a warrant and went to jail that day, but I was released."

At the time, Washburn lived in a house in the exclusive Atlanta suburb of Woodstock, but he wasn't there much. He was usually in the projects, getting high on drugs. One day, he went on a drug binge. It lasted a week.

CHRIS WASHBURN: "I was hanging with the boys in the projects doing crack, and I guess somebody got my house key and made a copy. When I stopped getting high, I decided it was time to go home, maybe change clothes after living four or five days in the same clothes. When I went home, I couldn't find the key to unlock the door. I had to get the spare key I had hidden in a flowerpot. When I opened the door, I was floored. There was nothing in my house, no furniture, no clothes, no refrigerator. They had taken everything from my house. They had kept me high in the projects. Meanwhile, they had robbed me blind. Even my trash disposal was gone.

"Another reason I returned home was that I needed to feed my dogs. I owned six Rottweilers. I had paid $5,000 for each dog. I guess my neighbors called the city dog catcher about my dogs. They had ridden by and seen that the dogs had not been properly taken care or fed. There was a note on the door from the dog catcher to let me know that they had taken the dogs, and I could come to the pound and get them.

"I called the cops, but they didn't come to the house until the next morning. I was getting high when they knocked on the door. I wouldn't let them in. I was quiet until they went away.

"So, drugs were dominating my whole life then. I was just obsessed about getting my next high. I would sit on the floor on the edge of my Whirlpool tub in my empty house to smoke the crack crap. But I didn't care, as long as I could get high.

"The next thing I knew, my house was in foreclosure. I wasn't making the payments anymore. All my money was going toward drugs. I was still spending $1,200 to $1,500 a day, and sometimes more.

"I was spending a lot on other people as well. I wanted to be the life of the party. I wanted to make sure I had people around me. I was deep into addiction, but I felt good. Everything was gone, my house, my furniture, my dogs. Yet, strangely, it seemed like a burden had been lifted from me. I had more time to do drugs. I know. I know. I didn't have my shit together.

"I went to the bank and found out there was a freeze on my account. Uncle Sam had frozen my account because I hadn't paid my taxes. They had audited me, and I owed them thousands of dollars. That's where Bill McCandless, my new agent, came in. He got me back together financially.

"I couldn't take any money out of the bank. I had to pawn my jewelry to support my drug habit. Then I had to pawn my car and some other stuff. I pawned a $30,000 bracelet to buy $500 worth of drugs. When I went back to the pawn shop, they were still ripping me off. They wanted me to pay $1,000 or $1,500 to get the bracelet back. I'd be like, 'Nah. You just go and keep it.'

"Then one night I saw where some drug dealers had stashed some drugs. I went to their hiding place and stole the drugs. Then I went back to the apartment and gave my girlfriend at the time some of the drugs.

"Now a few days later, we get a knock at the door. It's the Georgia Bureau of Investigation. I was still getting high. They want to check the house for drugs. My girlfriend says fine. I was like, fine. My name isn't on anything. But they found a little bag of powder inside of a flowerpot that we had in our living room. I knew it was the bag that I gave her, and she admitted that it was hers.

"I thought they were going to take me to jail, but they took my girlfriend instead. She left me her debit card to help get her a bond. Being the drug user that I was, the first thing I did was to check to see how much money was in her account, it contained $14,000. I took $100 out and went and got high.

"My girlfriend still hasn't called me. So, a $100 turns into $300. Now she calls. She has a bond, so she wants me to come and get her. I tell her I'm on my way. But I go and get high again. She has to sit in jail another day. This goes on for about 10 days or so. She had to sit in jail for ten days, waiting for me to come and get her out. But I'm getting high instead. Every time I go to the bank and take out her money, I go and get high. Then one night I said to myself, 'Okay. I've gotten high enough. I have to go and get her out right quick.'"

"My girlfriend was pissed. She didn't wanna call her mom or her dad or anybody, but I guess they were starting to wonder what had happened to her. I don't know if they put a missing person's report out, but, eventually, she called her parents and told them the situation.

"One night, I went to my girlfriend's apartment. I tried the key, but it wouldn't work. The apartment was locked from the inside. How could that be? I kept trying to open the door. Eventually, the door cracked open, and there standing before me was my girlfriend's cousin, a big old guy, and her dad. They had come from Kansas. My girlfriend was from Wichita, Kansas.

"They let me in. The first thing they said was, 'Where's the car keys?'

'Your car is downstairs,' I said.

'Where's the credit card?' They asked.

I gave them the card.

'Do you have any clothes or personal stuff in the apartment?' the dad asked.

I said, 'Yeah, I got a few clothes back in the room.'

They said, 'Let's go get them.'

So, I went to the back to get my stuff with the two guys following me.

"After I got my belongings, they escorted me to the front door and told me don't ever come back. I had no place to go. I had to think. I remembered I had a girlfriend in Dallas, Texas. Her name was Michelle.

"I had met her while I was in New York City just before the draft. She was with a girlfriend, and they were meeting the girlfriend's boyfriend. I saw her and thought she was cute. I introduced myself, and we talked for a while. We exchanged numbers. After I got drafted, we went out on a couple dates, and then I had to go to California for a pre camp. We kept in touch and communicated periodically.

"While I was in California, I never called her because, at that time, I'd met Jessica. But we still communicated back and forth periodically. I was just talking with her as a friend. We weren't romantically involved at that time.

"I called and gave her a sad story. She took pity on me and told me to come and see her. I thought she was gonna fly me there when she said, 'yeah. I'll get you a ticket.' But it was a bus ticket. She sent it to me. I had to take the bus from Atlanta to Dallas. It would take me about two days. I would have taken my Mercedes, but I couldn't find it. They eventually found the car, maybe a month later, halfway between Georgia and Florida on the side of the highway.

"On the way from Atlanta to Dallas, we made a stop at a gas station in Philadelphia, Mississippi. I was really hungry, but I had no money, and the credit card had been taken from me by my girlfriend's dad. I went inside the gas station and started to steal some food. But I got caught. Now this is Philadelphia, Mississippi, the same city where three civil rights workers were murdered."

In June 1964, during the civil rights movement, three civil rights workers, James Chaney, Andrew Goodman, and Michael Schwerner, were abducted and murdered in Philadelphia, Mississippi. The three had been working with a campaign that was attempting to register African Americans in Mississippi to vote.

CHRIS WASHBURN: "I knew nothing about that kind of history until years later. Philadelphia was still a dangerous place for a Black man. I went to jail. It was almost like a Mayberry type jail. I was in there with two white officers.

One of the cops said to me: 'You know where you at, boy?'

'Not really,' I said.

'This is not a place to be stealing,' one of the cops said. 'Why are you stealing?'

I told them I hadn't eaten in a couple of days. I just wanted something to eat.

'Why didn't you ask somebody for food?'

'I didn't know anybody to ask.' I said.

"One of the cops told me, 'There's no buses out of Philadelphia tonight, so you're not getting out of here, and you're not wandering our streets. The bus only comes once a day. We'll make sure you're on it tomorrow. We want you out of our city.'"

"Later, I realized how lucky I was. The cops could have made me disappear like those three murdered civil rights workers.

"Meanwhile, Michelle was at the bus station in Dallas waiting for me. I couldn't make a phone call. I never showed up. Michelle's thinking I went somewhere and got high. Eventually, I made it to Dallas. I called her on a pay phone. and she came out to get me. I had to explain the situation to her. I kinda smoothed things out. She took me to her house.

"I was there for maybe about three or four days before I started to walk the streets. Actually, I was looking for drug areas. I didn't have to leave the neighborhood. The neighborhood was middle class, but the houses had people who were selling drugs. I'd ask people for directions, and they'd tell me the house to go to.

"Michelle had given me $40 or $50, and I spent it on drugs. She'd give me little more money, and I would the same thing. Then I started feeling funny about asking her for money. So, I started walking around the house, looking for things to pawn, things she might not miss. Michelle was living in her old family house. Most of her family had moved out, but I figured they would have left some things behind. I would look at things and see if there was any kind of value in them. If I thought they had value, I would take them to the pawnshop.

"I would go through drawers and find things like rings, bracelets, jewelry…things she wouldn't miss. What was funny was that anytime I got a pawn receipt, I would put the receipt back in the area from where I had taken the item.

"Then I started finding shotguns. Her dad was a big hunter. I started pawning guns, getting as much as $2,300 a gun. Eventually, either her daddy or her brother came for one of the guns, and it wasn't there. But a pawn ticket was there. Then he went looking for something else and found another pawn ticket.

"Eventually, I came back to the house, and Michelle, her dad and brother were there. They were clutching a handful of pawn tickets. They knew what I did with the guns. I told them I had some money coming in from an accident. I was planning on getting all their stuff back to them. I did have an accident, and I did get money from it. They said they would hold the money for me. They said they didn't want me to blow it. They gave me a $100. So, that evening, I went out and spent the money on drugs. I came back about two in the morning, and they gave me another $100. But eventually, they got tired of giving me money. I had come for it so many times. They gave me all of the money and said don't spend it all at once. I ended up spending all the money they gave me on drugs."

Spud Webb, a former teammate of Chris Washburn at NC State and the Atlanta Hawks, recalls meeting Washburn on the streets of Dallas.

SPUD WEBB: "He looked terrible. I didn't know whether to laugh or cry. I almost didn't recognize him. He had let himself go. He looked dirty. He had on clothes, but not the kind I usually saw him dressed in. He must have weighed four hundred pounds. I said 'Chris, what happened to you?' How could you let yourself go like that?'"

CHRIS WASHBURN: "In 1990, I had started to date Michelle. She became my girlfriend. She had one son, about three or four years old. We talked about my drug life. She wanted me to stop. I told her about John Lucas whom I had met when I was at the treatment center in Van Nuys. John had come out there with Quinn Buckner to visit with some of the NBA players in the program. John and I had a North Carolina connection. He was from Durham. I was from Hickory. We both had played in the ACC.

"John took an interest in me. He told me that if I could get my act together, I was young enough that I could play in the NBA again. I know he got other players in the league. Two players I know specifically were Roy Tarpley and another kid named Richie Dumas. I talked with Michelle about John's treatment center. I can't remember if I called or Michelle called John, but whoever did, he decided to take me in. John wanted me to come out. He said it wouldn't cost me any money.

"I wanted to change but in my way. I wanted to learn how to be a functioning addict. I didn't really wanna stop because I liked what I was doing. I just wanted to know how I could do it better and maybe get back into the NBA. I wanted two slices of cake and to eat both of them, so to speak. But the truth is I was getting tired of the lifestyle. Michelle's family and me were getting on each other's nerves. It was time to do something different."

John Lucas knew well what it was to be down and out and a drug addict. In the mid-1970s, Lucas was a super-talented athlete who excelled in both basketball and tennis. He was an all-American in both sports at the University of Maryland. He was the No. 1 overall pick by the Rockets in the 1976 NBA draft. He had three stints with the Rockets in a 14-year career including stops with the Golden State Warriors, Washington Bullets, San Antonio Spurs, Milwaukee Bucks, and Seattle Super Sonics.

Lucas struggled with drug and alcohol addiction, and it nearly destroyed him. He went public with his addiction after being repeatedly suspended. Lucas voluntarily submitted to anti-drug and anti-alcohol treatment and managed to stay in the NBA.

In 1986, Lucas opened a Houston-based wellness and aftercare program that offers a substance abuse recovery program for athletes. Professional athletes, celebrities, and public figures have found success in Lucas' program. Several basketball players have gone through the program, including players who are veterans of the NBA and casualties of the War on Drugs, including Ken Bannister (New York Knicks, L.A. Clippers), Grant Gondrezick (Phoenix Suns, Clippers), Duane Washington (New Jersey Nets), Michael Graham (Seattle Supersonics). Patients give up their cellphones, cash, and keys, check into a Houston-area rehabilitation center for 30 days to detox, and then work out with Lucas to release stress and learn how to develop behavioral skills.

JOHN LUCAS: "Chris had just gotten suspended from the NBA, and he came to see me. I did not really know Chris. I knew he went to North Carolina State, and I knew he was from Hickory. At that time, the NBA was pretty heavily infested with drug abuse. I had just gotten to the other side and became one of the first athletes to maintain my sobriety. I opened a treatment center, and Chris eventually came. He was there for almost six months. He was one of the many NBA players who were at my center and who had been at risk through an addiction.

Chris was about 300 pounds, and then he began to lose weight and get into shape. We had three workouts a day. Besides playing basketball, we did a lot of sweating and conditioning to get some of the weight off of him. He had therapy. He had group sessions twice a week. He lived in our group home. That was solely for athletes. On the road, he roomed with a trainer to help him to kind of stay on track. I know he regressed, but it wasn't frustrating for me because only one out of ten athletes make it through the program. People like to tell me that I have had great luck. No, I haven't."

CHRIS WASHBURN: "I stayed a few weeks the first time I was there and ended up leaving and going on the streets again, the drugs called me back. I wasn't ready to stop. And so, I was in the streets of Houston for maybe a week or two weeks, before I actually came back to Lucas's facility.

"I must confess I stole money from John. I took money out of his little Louis Vuitton bag. I know that he knew I took it. It was embarrassing. I stole money from the person who's trying to help me. The second time I stole from John he had gone on a trip. He had a nice stereo in his office. I had security let me into John's office, and I took the stereo. I told the security guard it was my stereo."

JOHN LUCAS: "He pawned the stereo, but left me a note, telling me, thank you for holding my stereo. Haha! To this day, I have that note framed and hanging in his office to show people how strong drugs are."

When Washburn left Lucas' treatment center, he was actually living on the same street that John's facility was on.

CHRIS WASHBURN: "I was hanging at the far end, and the hospital, which contained John's facility, was toward the top of the street. I could actually stand in the middle of the street and look all the way down the road and see the hospital. That's just how close I was to it.

"I was sleeping in a carport. I would find me a car in the corner of the carport, get behind it and go to sleep. I lived like that when I was out in the street. At that time, I was eating out of garbage cans. Sometimes I would get a little money and go to a Chinese buffet that was on the same street. I would panhandle to get some money, and I would go on in and sit all day and just try to eat until they would tell me it was time for me to leave.

"I didn't have anywhere to go. So, after a while, I decided to go back to treatment. John took me back. He knows drug addiction. He had gone through it himself. He knew how powerful cocaine was. John let me come back to the point where I think I even finished that program. And when I got out, he got me an apartment and brought Michelle to live with me. We just had our first son, Julian. I was supposed to go to meetings and do the things that were needed. But what I ended up doing was leaving. Michelle and my son stayed, and I went back out on the street to get high.

"I ran across a guy I had been getting high with. I thought maybe I could have a hit and return to my apartment. But it wasn't one hit, and I didn't go back to the apartment.

"It was the same old scene except my friend had a car, and we went to a different area of Houston. Drug users on the street knew who I was. They wanted to be around me. I was getting free drugs. I wasn't ready to go home, but Michelle told me that if I wasn't coming back to the apartment Michelle would have to leave because the housing was for the people in the program. John didn't want me to go to the program in Houston. He had just opened up another facility in Fort Worth, and he wanted me to go there.

"I went to Fort Worth. I was out there a few weeks, and I just didn't like it. So, I left the program again. I was on the streets again, and I called a guy who had graduated from John's program. He had given me his number. He came and picked me up. He was staying at a motel called the Cadillac Inn. I thought I was gonna stay for a day and then leave. He had a little cocaine. I had a few dollars. He sold me some cocaine.

"I'm enjoying myself. He's waiting on me to leave, but I have nowhere to go. I'm sleeping on his floor. I was there for about a week when he decided to take me to Dallas. I went back to the crack house I knew in Dallas. I called Michelle to let her know I'm trying to get back to Houston for treatment. I told her to let John know."

Washburn would eventually be in treatment at John Lucas' clinic four times, but he finally left the program. At this time, Washburn thought he could still play pro basketball and decided he would join the Continental Basketball Association (CBA).

Before the G-League, the NBA had the CBA with teams stretching from Puerto Rico to Honolulu. The CBA's heyday was the 1980s and 90s, when the league provided a launching pad for future NBA All-Stars, such as John Starks and Michael Adams, as well as coaching legends Phil Jackson and George Karl.

The league was also the destination of last resort for faded stars, such as Roy Tarpley, John Drew, Lloyd Daniels, Michael Ray Richardson, and, of course, Chris Washburn. The CBA, which often billed itself as the "World's Oldest Pro Basketball League," operated from 1945 to 2009, pre-dating by two months, the founding of the National Basketball Association.

Washburn decided he would play for Tulsa Fast Breakers. The team took its name from Larry Stone's Fast Break Convenient Store and lasted three years (1988-89/1991-1992). They were league champions in 1989 and eventually changed their name to Tulsa Zone. Washburn signed with the Fast Breakers in late January 1991.

At the time of his signing, Washburn said that he looked at playing with the Fast Breakers as a stepping-stone to getting back in the NBA. Today, he says something different.

CHRIS WASHBURN: "The CBA didn't have the same kind of rules as NBA did, and so I was able at that time to get an opportunity to go there and play. Bill McCandless, my agent, has a good name and long arms, and he got the opportunity for me. Tulsa needed a big man. I was down from over 300 pounds to 285 pounds, a weight I could manage. But at the time, I wasn't thinking about getting back in the NBA. Playing basketball at the time wasn't the main thing for me. What I really wanted was not basketball but the NBA perks."

9

BROKEN DREAMS

"I wasn't gonna play because I liked basketball or to get my name out there. I needed to play because I needed the money. I had an expensive habit, a drug habit, and I had a growing family to support. Basketball was all I knew how to do." ~ Chris Washburn

When Chris Washburn was released from John Lucas' drug treatment center in January 1991, he had spent seven months in the program. Washburn told the press he had been sober the previous five months. Today, Washburn adds a twist to that story.

CHRIS WASHBURN: "Yeah, I was sober in the Lucas treatment facility, but once I was on the street again, it wasn't too long before I was back using. At the same time I was working on getting myself back with my wife because we had split up. That's why I was still on the streets in Houston. I couldn't go to Dallas because I hadn't made any changes, so she didn't want me to come to Dallas."

Washburn had not played professional basketball since the end of the 1987-88 season when he played in thirty-seven games for the Golden State Warriors and Atlanta Hawks and was subsequently banned from the league. He would be eligible to reapply for reinstatement into the NBA on March 21, 1991. Meanwhile, he had been cleared to play in the CBA.

The league was willing to take him. Irv Kaze, the league's commissioner, said in a statement, "He (Chris Washburn) has gone through an excellent rehabilitation and after-care program at the John Lucas Center, which is a tremendous facility. We feel that Chris is entitled to another shot.'"

Washburn had spent two months at the Lucas Center before going through thirty-five days of treatment. He then spent the last 120 days in outpatient care. Lucas arranged that Washburn would continue treatment at Century Health Care in Tulsa.

Washburn had the desire, a kind of long-term plan, or rather a wish, to make it back to the NBA. But deep down, he was happy with the lifestyle he was leading, and he did not want to work hard to achieve his long-term goal.

CHRIS WASHBURN: "I just wasn't all in at that time. But I did want to go and play in the NBA because of the lifestyle. I loved spending the money. I loved the glamor. But I wasn't that interested in working hard to get it. What I really wanted was to live in the world of the NBA player and in the world of the drug addict and survive and thrive in both worlds."

Basketball would not give up on Washburn. He had plenty of chances to attain the level of play that could get him back to living the lifestyle of the NBA player he so desired. Larry Stone, the owner of the CBA Tulsa Fast Breakers, decided to take the risk and signed Chris Washburn to a contract that made him the highest-paid player in the CBA.

CHRIS WASHBURN: "John Lucas helped to arrange the deal with the Breakers because I didn't have an agent at the time. All I did was respond positively to a call that said I was going to Tulsa. Arrangements were made, and I went down there. They had a furnished apartment set up for me."

Accompanying Washburn was Jim Price, a former collegiate coach who had been with Fast Breakers as a volunteer assistant coach. Price would serve a familiar role, a minder who would live with Washburn and travel with the team on the road. Price and Washburn shared an apartment and went to Cocaine Anonymous meetings together. Washburn's urine was randomly tested twice a week. Washburn did not mind the arrangement.

CHRIS WASHBURN: "I knew I had a bad addiction, and a lot of the newspapers that were reporting on me said I would be dead before I was twenty-five because of the areas I was hanging in and the things that I was doing. It wasn't an unfamiliar situation having someone go with me. At Golden State, I had Greg Ballard and at NC State Dereck Whittenburg."

It was quite a deal since Washburn had not played basketball for a while. He had let himself go. He had not been exercising and was overweight. His condition was a lot lower than the accepted NBA standard.

Tulsa had a good team that was coached by Henry Bibby, a good friend of John Lucas. Bibby had played for the NBA's New York Knicks, New Orleans Jazz, Philadelphia 76ers, and San Diego Clippers. He would coach the Fast Breakers from 1987 to 1991.

CHRIS WASHBURN: "Coach Bibby was okay. I liked the arrangement because it was my second chance to play for a Black coach. I came to the Breakers in midseason, so I didn't really get a chance to know him because the season was already underway."

Washburn's performance with the Breakers was mediocre, except for one game in February against the Colombus (Ohio) Horizon before a season-high crowd of 5,159. Washburn finished with season-high stats of twenty-three points and twelve rebounds in thirty-nine minutes.

Washburn showed flashes of his former self in the game. Midway through the first quarter, Washburn stole the ball, drove the length of the court using a cross-over dribble to get by the Colombus guard, and scored a layup. Then, in the fourth quarter, he took an inbounds pass, faked handing the ball to a teammate, and drove the baseline for a spectacular dunk.

CHRIS WASHBURN: "I thought I was coming back. Then coach Bibby benched me. It was really frustrating. I wasn't being given a chance."

Bibby complained publicly and vocally about Washburn's work ethic—or lack of it—in the press. Washburn concedes that there might have been truth to Bibby's criticism.

CHRIS WASHBURN: "I was probably not working like an NBA person should've been working, that is, not giving it my all. I was trying to get by, to get in the groove of things, back into better shape."

Bibby did not bring Washburn with the team for the next game, the season finale in Wichita Falls. Chris Washburn, the highest-paid player in the CBA, averaged just 7.7 points and 4.6 rebounds in twenty games since signing with the Fast Breakers.

CHRIS WASHBURN: "I agree now that I wasn't doing my best, but back then, no, I didn't agree. I thought I was doing everything possible to play at my best 'cause I was still able to score. I thought I was still able to play."

As the Fast Breakers bounded into the playoffs, Washburn's playing status was still uncertain. The Fast Breakers finished the season with a 31-25 record. The team's season ended when the Santa Barbara Islanders won their best-of-five series with the Fast Breakers 3-2 with a 121-116 victory in the final game.

Washburn left Tulsa disappointed. He and his wife went back to Houston, Texas, to live in an apartment Lucas provided for him. Washburn still had some money from his contract with the Fast Breakers. It was not too long before he was back on the street looking for and using drugs.

CHRIS WASHBURN: "I was doing more drugs now than probably at any time in my life. I'm doing dumb things. I'm going into abandoned places and smoking. Police are starting to notice me now a lot more because of my size."

On July 6, 1991, police arrested Washburn at a Houston apartment after finding a crack pipe near him. Washburn claimed he had just stopped by to pick up some T-shirts and didn't know the crack pipe was near him. At the time, Washburn complained that he wasn't allowed to submit to a drug test, but it was pointed out to him that he was arrested for possession, not use.

He posted bail and was given a court-appointed attorney. He was ordered to be present at 9 a.m. on a certain date for his trial. He never showed up. Washburn's attorney appealed to the judge to give him another chance. He'll be here tomorrow at nine sharp, the attorney assured the judge. Washburn showed up this time, rolling in about twenty-five minutes late.

The judge was upset. She revoked his bail and put him back in jail. Washburn would spend eighty-nine days waiting for his trial. In October, the jury took seven and a half hours to convict Washburn. The prosecution had asked for at least a five-year sentence. Washburn asked for probation so he could continue playing basketball, the livelihood he needed for himself and his family.

"I am a lot older. I understand my position," Washburn told the judge. "Also, I have a child on the way and I'm trying to settle down and raise a family. I have a chance to play basketball, and I know it's more of a privilege to play than just something to do."

Washburn would appeal and lose the decision. It was not until 1994, however, that he would go to jail.

Meanwhile, in early August 1991, John Lucas bought the Miami Tropics basketball team as a tool for helping players overcome drug problems. The purchase price for the team was not disclosed. The team would play a twenty-game summer schedule.

Before Lucas bought the Tropics, the team had a shaky history. It did win the USBL championship in 1987, its first year in the league, but the next year, it folded after playing all but seven games of their thirty-game schedule, putting the team roughly $78,000 in debt. The season prior to the Lucas purchase, the Tropics survived front-office turnover and a mid-season coaching change to reach the finals.

CHRIS WASHBURN: "At the time I was in Houston. John was coming up with the idea of putting a basketball team together. We had twelve or thirteen players at John's clinic, enough for an entire team. John let us know that the team he was organizing was coming up with would play in the USBL. He would call the team the Miami Tropics.

"I had never been to Florida. I would listen to the older guys talk about the cocaine, the drugs that they've done in Florida and stuff like that. So now I'm ready to go to Florida, but I'm not ready to go to Florida for basketball. I'm really wanting to go for the drugs."

The USBL (United States Basketball League) was a professional men's spring basketball league that formed in 1985 and ceased operations in 2008. The USBL started in 1985 as one of the first basketball leagues to play a late-spring to early-summer schedule. The league became known as a development league for players, with many players moving up to the National Basketball Association (NBA) and many more playing in Europe.

Seven of the individuals who would play for the team would have a history of drug problems. In addition to Washburn, they included Roy Tarpley, Duane Washington, Richard Dumas, and Grant Gondrezick.

Roy Tarpley was a high-profile, troubling case. He had briefly played in the NBA. He was already doing drugs and alcohol at a rapid pace, but he still managed to look like a potential perennial All-Star.

Tarpley played for the Dallas Mavericks from 1986 to 1991. During the 1989–90 season, he was arrested six games in for driving under the influence and resisting arrest, leading to an NBA suspension. In March 1991, he faced another suspension after being arrested for DWI once again. Later that year, after a third offense, he was banned from the league for breaking the NBA's drug-use rules.[8]

CHRIS WASHBURN: "Roy did some crack, but his biggest thing was alcohol. He liked to drink a lot. He was

8. "Roy Tarpley," Wikipedia, November 6, 2024, https://en.wikipedia.org/wiki/Roy_Tarpley.

an alcoholic. I was never a drinker. I watched my dad as I grew up, and I knew what alcohol could do to you. It's kinda ironic given my history with cocaine.

"Anyway, I was trying to see why they are giving this guy all this praise. When I get to practice, Roy shows me. He was a little bigger than me, but he had good handles and a nice shot. I could see why he could be the sixth man of the year. Roy could play."

Lucas brought his team to Miami and they stayed at Florida International University. There was a section of the college that was blocked off for the team to live in. There were no students there.

Washburn was hoping to lose weight, wanting to trim down to 265 pounds. He had gone from 315 pounds to 285 prior to joining the Tropics, but Lucas wanted Washburn to go even lower to 250 pounds.

The talent-rich Tropics jumped off to a good start, going six and zero before losing to the Philadelphia Spirit 126-117. The Tropics played without its leading scorer, Roy Tarpley, who missed the game because of a stiff shoulder. Washburn played in place of Tarpley, scored six points, and pulled down four rebounds.

The Tropics would lose three more games before reaching the finals of the USBL championship on July 12, 1992. The Tropics faced the tough Philadelphia Spirit, with which they had split four games during the regular season. The Tropics survived seven ties and eight lead changes in the fourth quarter and had to score in the last four seconds to garner a close 116-114 victory and the championship.

Duane Washington, who was with the NBA's New Jersey Nets when he failed a drug test in 1988, led the 24-4 Tropics with thirty-two points and was named Most Valuable Player.

Washburn was the only player who did not make it to the final game. He had been suspended for violating team rules.

CHRIS WASHBURN: "What happened was Richie Dumas and me went out on the town the night after a practice. Richie liked to drink, and we went out for some beer. We had some crack on us, so we found a place in the projects to smoke it. We ran out of crack. We wanted some more, so we found the guys who had sold us the crack. We didn't have enough money on us, so they sold us the crack on credit... about $500 to $600 worth.

"Now we already missed curfew, but we had to get back to the team for practice. We had run up a tab with those guys for the crack. We told the dealers we'd be back. They said, 'Wait a minute. You owe us money. We need to go to practice with you.' None of the practices had been open to the public, but they insisted and followed us to the practice. The gym is closed, but the two dudes got in and are sitting in the stands. John spots the dealers and walks over to them. He tells them the practice is closed. 'What are you doing here?' They point to Richie and me. 'They owe us money,' they say. 'Not until they pay us, do we leave.'

"They argue. Finally, John relented and paid them. John was angry with us. But Richie is the leading scorer on the team, probably our best player. He's playing good. Me not so good. So, he suspends me and keeps Richie on the team."

Today, Lucas remembers the incident and marvels at the situations in which Washburn found himself and how risky his lifestyle was.

JOHN LUCAS: "Some of the situations he found himself in were just incredible. At that time, he almost got us all killed because those drug dealers came to one of our sessions looking for Chris because Chris owed them money. I remember putting him on the plane, seeing the gate close and watching his big ass get on the plane and out of there. But you know what? I never gave up on him. He would always be apologetic, sorry, remorseful, even when he took my stereo."

While Washburn was dealing with his suspension, he learned some sad news. On April 28, 1993, Jim Valvano, his coach at NC State, died at the Duke University Medical Center. Valvano had battled bone cancer for two months. Valvano never had a losing season. His underdog Wolfpack team won the 1983 NCAA championship game in a thrilling victory against the University of Houston.

CHRIS WASHBURN: "I went to the funeral. I was surprised to see only a few players show up. I really wanted to thank him for the time he spent with me. When I left State, I did not get a chance to talk to him anymore."

Valvano was well respected and well-liked, but his downfall came when Peter Golenbock published his *Personal Fouls* book in July 1989. Although much of the claims against Valvano were unsubstantiated, Valvano was fired.

One of the claims of Golenbock's book was that Washburn was a cocaine user at North Carolina State. Claire Lightner, a girlfriend of Washburn's at NC State, who had a baby with him, says she never saw Washburn use cocaine at NC State.

CLAIRE LIGHTNER: "Chris wasn't using cocaine when he was at NC State. I never saw him use it. All he would do is the casual stuff, marijuana."

CHRIS WASHBURN: "I never read the Golenbock's book, but then again, like I said, after I left the school, you know, they had another little scandal come up with tennis shoes. Golenbock had me on the (1983) championship team, and then he also had me involved with the tennis shoe scandal.

So, I don't know how I can attend NC State for six years when I was only there for two."

Valvano was fired from coaching at N.C. State, which incurred a 1989-90 ban on postseason participation and a two-year NCAA probation for longstanding failure to police the sale of game tickets and athletic shoes worn by basketball players. Valvano negotiated a settlement with NC State and resigned as basketball coach on April 7, 1990.

After his disappointing tenure with the Tropics in Miami, Washburn stayed in Houston with his wife and son. He went to live in an apartment provided by John Lucas. He had a little money in his pocket and went back on the street to his old ways, looking for his next fix.

The previous February 7, 1993, Washburn had gotten married to his girlfriend, Michelle. The wedding was nothing special.

CHRIS WASHBURN: "The wedding wasn't even formal. It was just my wife and cousin, who was a pastor and married us. He came to our place on his way to church. I had just come home from a binge, about a three-day binge, and my wife and the pastor woke me up. I got married in my underwear in the front room. Our neighbor came over and served as the best man. My wife had threatened to leave me. We were going to have our second child, and we weren't married."

Despite another setback, Washburn still believed he could play. Besides, it was all he knew to do. He had never really worked like your average Joe at a 9 to 5 job.

CHRIS WASHBURN: "I wasn't gonna play because I liked basketball or to get my name out there. I wanted to play because I needed the money. I had an expensive habit, a drug habit, and I had a growing family to support. Basketball was all I knew how to do."

All Chris Washburn wanted, however, was crack cocaine.

One day, while coming home from school, thirteen-year-old Nick Williams saw a big, tall Black man lumbering down the street. The Black man was the tallest man he had ever seen. It was Chris Washburn. He watched Washburn stroll into his mother Margaret's beauty shop. Nick went across the street and entered his mother's salon. Washburn was panhandling.

CHRIS WASHBURN: "When I left the Tropics, I returned to Houston and was on the street again. That's when I met Margaret. It was almost the Christmas holidays, and I was doing a lot of stealing from stores because they were putting out those big perfume bundles and I needed the money. My mother had stopped sending me money. My wife had gone back to Dallas. She was tired of my street ways and having to support me. I was an embarrassment to her. I had no way of making money.

"I can still remember the perfume brand: Elizabeth Taylor, White Diamond. The stall for these perfumes where near the store's exit door. So I would just walk in and grab some of the perfume bundles and run out. Then I'd tried to sell them on the street for half price. I would get about $50 or $60 a packet.

"I would go into Margaret's beauty salon and sell the perfume to her. I did that a couple of times. Then one day she said she wasn't gonna buy anymore from me. Instead, she was gonna take me home with her and get me straight.

NICK WILLIAMS: "My mother kicked Chris out of the shop and told him, 'Don't come back until you need some help.' And he ended up coming back, and one day ended on the couch with my uncle. Both of them had drug problems. Chris was pretty strung out back then. But he was like a big kid. We would play basketball, and he'd come by and shoot baskets with me.

"One day, Chris was driving us to school when we had a bad car accident. It was a head on collision. Me, Chris, and my brother Wayne were in the car. We all got injured, and we had to go to the chiropractor and the doctors. I missed a lot of the basketball season that year. But Chris, told me, 'Don't worry about it. You're gonna get paid. The person who hit us was in the wrong.' And we did get a settlement."

CHRIS WASHBURN: "Because I had a license, I could take the kids to school. I had been doing that for a little while. Unfortunately, we got into a wreck. We went to the hospital and had the kids checked out. I knew we'd get some money. I hadn't had any money coming in. Everybody had their own claim. I ended up getting $6,000."

The bond between Washburn and Nick and his family remains strong today.

NICK WILLIAMS: "Chris is part of our family to this day. I will say, though, that he's been really lucky. He was famous, but he hung around the projects. He hung around some of the worst people, and he is still alive."

One day, Washburn was on the phone with Michelle, trying to talk her into coming back to him. He put Margaret on the phone with Michelle, and Margaret told her Chris was doing fine. He was even going to church a couple of times a week. The weeks went by, and Washburn and Michelle continued to talk. Finally, Michelle said she would come and see Chris.

CHRIS WASHBURN: "She came from Dallas to see me. She could see I was making some changes. We decided I would leave with her. I grabbed all my stuff and went outside. I'd already received the check from the insurance company. We went back to Dallas. The first couple of days I'm fine. I'm in the house doing whatever I have to do with the kids. Michelle is out of the house doing whatever she needs to do with work.

"Then I start my walking around. I have maybe a $100 in my pocket the first day, and I might come home with that $100. I still got money in my pocket, but I'm buying drugs, and it all changes. I run through the money I had…around $6,000 that could've lasted us a couple months. My wife's not working. We need money. The only skill and talent I have is pro basketball."

Remarkably, despite all the problems and his growing reputation as a drug addict, Washburn would get yet another call to return to basketball. This time, it would be the Westchester Stallions, a new team in the USBL just starting up. Westchester County is located close to New York City, just north of the Bronx, and is actually considered a suburb of New York City.

Westchester County had shown a reluctance to support a local team. An organization known as the Westchester Hoops Inc. believed this time it would be different. The organization backed the Stallions with a 15-member management team with a sophisticated marketing plan and a willingness to spend $500,00 over the next two years.

Marc Washington, who was the Stallion's general manager, explained how the team recruited Chris Washburn.

MARC WASHINGTON: "After we had four or five internal meetings about Chris, we decided to have a come to Jesus conversation with him. We were aware of his drug problems because I had spoken with people in the NBA and everybody else, and so we did as much due diligence as we could. We decided that if he could stay sober, we should give him a chance. And so, we started talking with Chris and Michelle, and we decided to give him a chance. It would be up to him to earn it.

"We told Chris we would put safeguards around him, that he would not be alone. If the team traveled, there would be people with him. We sent his paycheck to Michelle.

"All he had to do was wake up, stay straight, be focused, and lose weight because, when he walked into our office, he was 315 pounds. I told him our job is to get you down to maybe 275 or 280. We did get him down a bunch. And he did everything he was supposed to do up until about eight to nine or ten weeks later when that unfortunate occurrence with Marty Eggleston happened.

The Stallions management had high hopes for Chris Washburn, who showed up in Westchester, but he was a far cry from the talented Washburn Golden State who had drafted third in the 1986 draft. Seth Davis, a reporter with the Connecticut *New Haven Register* newspaper, described what he saw when he watched Washburn take the court:

Davis wrote bluntly: "They might see Chris Washburn....but they won't recognize him." Davis wrote: "He is overweight and slow afoot—not nearly the powerful, imposing presence inside he once was as a star at North Carolina State."

Davis described Washburn's performance in a game against the Connecticut Sky Hawks in which he only played a few minutes: "He didn't run the floor well at all. He drove to the basket only once, missing badly because he had no quickness in his legs. He scored on a hook shot and was replaced early, visibly tired."

In early May 1993, the Stallions signed and activated him. Washburn's stay with the Stallions was stunningly short.

CHRIS WASHBURN: "I was excited about getting another chance, but there was a big guy on the team named Marty Eggleston. He was out of Philadelphia. About seven feet, a big guy. One day, he was mouthing off to me, telling me how bad I was playing, how bad I made the NBA look, and so forth. We were in the bathroom. I was drinking a beer, feeling bad. Finally, he said, 'Look at you. drinking a beer. Don't you have any discipline.'

"I looked at him, and he looked at me. I had it. I jumped up and smacked him on the head with a forty-ounce bottle, stunning him. I dashed into my room, locked the door. I thought I was safe, but he went nuts, tried to break the door down. And I'm glad he never succeeded because he's a little bit bigger than me.

"He tried but couldn't get into the room. The owners then came, settled him down, got him to the hospital. He needed some stitches. They then told me that I needed to pack my stuff up. I was off the team."

MARK WASHINGTON: "I walked in after the ruckus, and the bathroom looked like Beirut. The work men and the security guards, no one was going in, which was good. And what I got from the two of them when I interviewed each of them separately was that Marty had been in a sour mood and came at Chris. Chris hit him with a bottle in his face, opening it up, and he had to get a bunch of stitches.

"And so, from that moment on, to everyone's credit, to his teammates' credits, to the assistant coaches and everybody, cooler heads prevailed, and we came to the understanding that both Chris and Marty could not be part of the organization anymore. So, we essentially fired them.

"We eventually took Chris to the airport to go home. I told him I was proud of him. The incident with Marty was a difficult situation, but if you can continue to stay on the path and try to be the best version of yourself that you can be, you will be alright. He said he would. And I said I loved him, and he said he loved me, and then he went home."

In early June, the Stallions released Washburn, no explanation given to the public. It was yet another setback in the still relatively young hoopster's career.

CHRIS WASHBURN: "In my drugged mind, I thought I would play again. But I continued to think I could live in both worlds. I just couldn't accept the fact that playing basketball was no longer my main focus."

Washburn's troubles continued to pile up. He was arrested at a Dallas residence on August 13, accused of using a friend's credit card without permission to pay for a room at a motel in late July.

On September 7, a Tarrant County grand jury indicted Chris Washburn on a felony charge of using a stolen credit card to pay for about a week of his room charges. Police revealed that when he had also tried to get money back from the motel for days charged in advance, the motel clerk got suspicious and called the police. The police called the card's owner who said Washburn was not authorized to use the card. The bond was set at $50,000.

Police dropped the fraudulent use of a credit charge against Washburn, and he was released from a Fort Worth jail, only to be arrested again on October 22. This time, he was charged with seven counts of forgery and one count of misdemeanor larceny. He was held on a $10,500 secured bond.

Washburn decided to return to Hickory. Michelle, who would later become Chris's wife, decided to leave for Dallas.

CHRIS WASHBURN: "Michelle's brother came to help move her back to Dallas. I helped to carry some of the furniture out of the apartment. I gave her a hug and said I was going to get my act together. The apartment was cleaned out except for some of my clothes.

"I remember after they left and looking out the window and seeing them go down the street. I sat on the floor because all the furniture was gone, the apartment empty. In the empty apartment. I sat on the floor crying. I had nowhere to go. I could have gone back to the Lucas treatment center, but I decided against it. I called my parents in Hickory, and they took me back in.

"My mom was good with me. She would send me money. But when I returned to Hickory, she about had it with me. She wouldn't give me any more money. I had burned the bridge to my mom. She just told me to put my name and my number in my pocket, so when they find my body, they'll at least know where to send the body."

When Washburn returned to Hickory, nothing in his lifestyle changed.

CHRIS WASHBURN: "I was still going to the abandoned houses to smoke crack. I was still looking in garbage cans. I was doing the same thing in Hickory as I was doing in Houston because I didn't how to change. My addiction followed me, hounded me, and whatever came with the addiction also followed me."

Washburn came back to Hickory with his addiction, but he could not escape trouble. He was accused of taking a purse from an employee at a Hickory doctor's office in August and cashing personal checks found in the purse. A woman's wallet was stolen from a Hickory office The woman spotted Washburn leaving the office. The checks were cashed at a Winn-Dixie grocery store for a total of $648, used for food and cash, Hickory police said.

"Washburn told Hickory police earlier this week he was going to be in town, and he wanted to turn himself in," said Lt. Ronny Lamberth with the Hickory Police Department. But when he didn't show up on a Thursday, authorities went looking for him. He was arrested around 2:30 a.m. in Hickory near the Sunny Valley Apartments, which was located close to the police department's satellite station.

Mike Chris was a Hickory Police Department officer who met Chris in the mid-1990s while driving a black Mercedes. He had parked it in a well-known drug spot and high-crime-area.

MIKE CHRIS: "I saw this big ass guy get out of that Mercedes, and I said, 'who the hell is that' I learned he was Chris Washburn, a famous basketball player. He had played at North Carolina State and then washed out in the NBA, Later, he flagged me down and said someone to whom he had loaned his car had not given it back. I eventually found his car, but I would take notice of him after that. He was just too big."

Chris concedes he could have arrested Washburn a couple of times, but he says Washburn is such a nice guy that he had to let him go.

MIKE CHRIS: "One night I was riding down the street and saw a big guy in a parking lot. I cut my lights off and whipped in to the parking lot. Chris was too big to run, so he just stood there. I took a crack pipe off of him and drove him home."

Other Hickory police officers were not as accommodating. In early December, Washburn was arrested and charged with cocaine possession. Police found a rock of crack on Washburn when they searched him outside a convenience store. A police officer saw a transaction between Washburn and another man. The other man was not arrested because no drugs were found on him. Washburn was put in jail under a $1,500 secured bond. Washburn was given probation.

Remarkably, in 1994, Washburn was given another chance to play basketball when John Lucas invited him back to the Miami Tropics. Instead of putting Washburn in the team house, Lucas placed him with players who had their own apartments. They included coach Kevin Mackay, Dexter Manley, and Reggie Cobb. They were two-bedroom apartments, so when Washburn left, his roommate would know about it. Washburn, however, would find some way to slip out and search for drugs.

Washburn would end up not playing a minute for the Tropics. In early June 1994, Washburn was suspended not for drugs, but for loafing.

Dick Barth, a Tropics spokesperson, explained: "They thought for his own well-being, because he wasn't working hard on basketball, he would be better off getting away and going back home. They wanted him working as hard as any other player. He really wasn't working that hard."

The Tropics denied that Washburn had a drug problem despite the evidence. No, Washburn's problem, according to the Tropics, was laziness. He has to put out more of an effort.

CHRIS WASHBURN: "I ended up not playing for the team. If I was loafing, it was probably from doing drugs."

Chris Washburn had hit rock bottom. He had so many chances to shape up. Yet, he continued to do drugs and lead a reckless lifestyle. He had burned his bridges that led back to the NBA. But he still wanted to play basketball. Where could he play? What team would be willing to take a chance on him?

10

OVERSEAS

"I was supposed to meet with the owners, I was in no shape at that point to meet anyone. I was strung out from the cocaine. When I didn't show up, they came looking for me. I hadn't changed clothes since arriving in Argentina. I must have looked like a mess." ~ Chris Washburn

In 1993, after failing to stick in the CBA and USBL, Chris Washburn returned to Hickory, continuing the life that he had led since being banned by the NBA.

Michelle had reconciled with Chris after she visited him in Houston and brought him back to Dallas to live with her. She followed Washburn to Hickory. Chris had run through the insurance money he received from the car accident, and the couple was broke. He had blown the money on drugs. Michelle was not working. She was at odds with her family because she had reconciled with Chris. The family thought that he was a bad influence on her, and they refused to help the couple. Fortunately, Michelle found a job. It was hard work and totally different than the office work she had been doing. She had been a manager for Sprint in New York City.

But she did it, and the Washburns survived financially. The couple moved in with Chris Washburn's parents.

CHRIS WASHBURN: "I was running the streets, getting high. I didn't really care about playing basketball. Hickory was not Atlanta or San Francisco. It's a small rural town. The hardest thing for me at that time in Hickory was to avoid people so they couldn't see what I was doing. I was trying to keep a low profile, but the drugs took over and trying to keep a low profile went out the window. It's hard to be inconspicuous in Hickory.

"I still had the status of a pro athlete. People still wanted to take pictures, still wanted autographs. I would take a picture or give an autograph, and then I'd ask for some money. I would never ask for money directly. I would say something like: 'Can I borrow $20' or something like that? I'd always borrow.

"It was a change for me. When I was playing, I had the money to buy drugs and bring them to Hickory with me. So, I wouldn't have to be on the streets. I would get a hotel room, invite some friends over, I wouldn't have to run the streets. But I was broke, so I had to be out on the streets, and being the big guy that I am, along with my reputation, it was hard to be anonymous."

The basketball world had not forgotten about Chris Washburn. He would get another basketball playing opportunity, not from the U.S. but from overseas.

Washburn's agent, Bill McCandless, called Washburn to tell him that there was an opening in Greece.

The team he would play for was PAOK BC, which was based in Thessaloniki, the second-largest city in Greece. The PAOK basketball club did well in European competition earning it a stellar reputation in Greek pro basketball. The trip, however, turned out to be a disappointment. Washburn lasted three days.

CHRIS WASHBURN: "It was actually a good paying gig. The quality of play was A level. I'm thinking I may be too fat to play in the NBA, but I should be able to play in this league. It's going to be good money. I gotta go over there and play."

But Washburn's drug-induced life was taking its toll on him. In the last couple of years, he has not taken care of himself. He had not exercised or worked out regularly. He weighed close to 400 pounds and had a hard time making it down the court. But he needed the money, so Washburn remained optimistic.

CHRIS WASHBURN: "I went out to eat one time. I went to just one practice. I got in that evening, practiced one day, stayed the next day, and then left the next morning. The team's management took me aside and told me that I was out of shape and that they no longer needed me. They said I showed up a lot bigger than what they were told.

"I think I pissed them off, too. After that one practice, they said I had to go on a cross-country run. I told them, 'Yeah, but I don't do no running. I just want to relax after practice.' Actually, what I really wanted to do was drugs. But the trip wasn't a total waste. They paid me about $6,000. When I returned to the U.S., McCandless was angry with me. He said I wasn't serious enough and that he was wasting his time with me. He had other guys who were willing to play overseas and were serious about playing their way back to the NBA. So, he let me go. I no longer had an agent. Meanwhile, I went back to the street and my old ways."

One day, his mother got a phone call. It was from an agent in South Carolina named Jake Talley. He told Savannah that he wanted to come to Hickory and talk to Chris. She found him in the projects and relayed the message to him. Then Talley came to see Washburn. He was African American. Washburn had never had a Black agent interested in him before.

"Talley told me about all the things he'd done overseas with American players, the kind of money they were making and things like that. I was especially interested in the money. If I could get some money, I could keep buying drugs. He gave me some options about where I could go. He said he was gonna throw my name out there and see what would stick, if there were any takers. Jake came with a contract, and I signed it. He went back to South Carolina and began looking for a job for me overseas. He found me a gig in Argentina."

Washburn called Marc Washington to get his advice about going overseas once again to play basketball. He would have liked to call John Lucas, but their relationship had soured after he left the Tropics when Lucas suspended him for loafing.

MARK WASHINGTON: "Weeks after Chris left the Westchester Stallions, I got a call from him. He says to me, 'Coach, it's me. I've got an opportunity to play in Argentina.' I went through the basics with him. Are you straight? Are you doing what you need to do? Are you taking care of yourself? Are you staying away from the wrong people?' And he said he was, and we went back and forth and then the conversation ended.

"I got another call from him in which he said, 'I have a gentleman from the state department on the phone. He wants to verify that I worked for the Stallions.' The gentleman asked me a couple of questions, and I said, 'Yes, he's seeking employment through a basketball contract.' I think they were trying to make sure he wasn't a mule or some kind of crazy dude."

CHRIS WASHBURN: "Jake said it was a good assignment because they paid on time and would give me a little money up front. Of course, I liked that because I would be able to buy some drugs. "They bought me an airline ticket. It was first class. Everything about the assignment was first class. I flew to Buenos Aires.

"I didn't know anything about Argentina. It was really different. I couldn't speak the language, but I had an interpreter. In the evening, I would tell him to go home. I don't need you until tomorrow. I'm not going out tonight. He would go home, and that's when I would sneak out and go and find drugs.

"I remember one time I went to a restaurant and wanted to buy some chicken. They couldn't understand me. So, I started flapping my arms like a chicken. You know, chicken, man. Hahaha.

"I ran across this kid, and he was able to find me some cocaine without any problem. It seems the word "cocaine" is universal. So, I got settled and met with the team reps. They told me through the interpreter what was expected of me. They put me in an apartment above a store. If you've had experience with (illegal) drugs, like me, you know that when you go on the street you can spot the dealers. But in buying drugs, I had to be careful 'cause I didn't know the area, and I didn't know the dealers. I met a dealer. I didn't have any foreign money on me, so I had to give him American money. I gave him twenty-five American dollars. I didn't really know what the American dollar was worth. But wow! He gave me cocaine that looked like it was worth $300 to $400.

"I went to my room. I had to figure out how to smoke it because it didn't come in rock form. But I did figure it out, and I was in business. I spent the night smoking crack. And so, the next day came, and I was supposed to meet with the owners. I was in no shape at that point to meet anyone. I was strung out from the cocaine. When I didn't show up, they came looking for me. I hadn't changed clothes since arriving in Argentina. I must have looked like a mess.

"They took me out to eat, but I didn't have an appetite. The meeting didn't go well. I was still strung out. I went to a practice, but it didn't go well either. They told me they couldn't use me because I wasn't in shape. I can't remember the Spanish word for fat, but that's what they called me. They told me to change my diet. Less beer, more juices."

MARK WASHINGTON: "About two weeks after going to Argentina, Chris called me. He told me how good he was doing down there. I said, 'Chris, just stay on the path. You're doing everything right.' Then he called me about four or five weeks later and said, 'Coach, I'm not motivated. I wanna go home.' I told him, 'Christopher, you've made a path for yourself. You've come from the darkness into the light. Michelle and your children need your income, but more importantly, for yourself, you need stability, and you need a place to work. And then after that conversation, I didn't hear from him again for a long, long time."

CHRIS WASHBURN: "I don't know if the team in Argentina knew I was taking drugs. I don't know how much due diligence they did on me. The team in Argentina bought me a return ticket and within forty-eight hours I was out of the country. The good thing: I still had some money in my pocket.

"Jake wasn't really upset with me, but he said I had to get in shape. So, I started working out a little. But I had no guidance, and nobody to watch me and prod me. It wasn't long before I was back to my old ways."

Eventually Jake Talley came back with another proposition. He had found a team in Colombia.

CHRIS WASHBURN: "It was not as good a league as the one in Argentina, but Jack said we would have no problem getting paid. In fact, they sent me a couple of thousands of dollars in advance. The only problem was that they paid up front, about a week or so before I was to leave for Colombia. That sounds like a good idea, but by the time I was ready to go to Colombia. I was broke. I had spent the money on crack. If it wasn't for them paying for everything in Colombia, I would have been in serious financial trouble. I might have starved to death.

"When I arrived in Bogota, I was like a kid in the candy shop. It was so easy to find drugs. And cheap, too. For $25 in Colombia, I got more drugs than I had in Argentina. I was supposed to meet the team the next morning at practice, but I missed it. I was in no shape from the drug binge I went on the night before."

"Doing dope in Colombia is different than doing it in Argentina. This time, I had something to smoke with. I had brought a pipe with me. They had told me to be at practice the next day, I said, 'sure' and went out on the street looking for drugs. I found a guy, who for $25, gave me some cocaine wrapped in aluminum foil. He didn't have a plastic bag.

"I spent the whole night getting wasted, but I'm getting paranoid because I'm hearing things. Little sounds made me jumpy. If I dropped something on the floor in the past, I wouldn't look for it. Now I am on the floor trying to find it. I would sit in the corner for several minutes, just staring. Then I would go back doing drugs. I would stop and sit over in the corner for maybe about thirty or forty minutes, maybe even longer, until that high wore off, or the paranoia wore off, and then I would go back to doing the drugs again.

"I would push a chair up against the door and continue to get high. I would lose track of time and miss practice. They came to get me, but I wouldn't open the door for them. They banged and banged on the door, but I wouldn't answer. The next morning, I leave my room because I'm out of drugs. I really wanna go out and find some more drugs. One of the team's assistants is there, and he says to me, 'Hey, are you alright?' 'Yeah,' I'd say. 'I was asleep all day. I guess the time got to me.'

Washburn returned to the U.S. thinking his basketball playing days were over, but incredibly, like the cat with nine lives, he would get another opportunity. This time it would be Switzerland.

CHRIS WASHBURN: "I flew to Zurich and then to Basel. I'm going to be playing in a different kind of league. I play just one game a week. That's okay with me because, again, I wasn't in shape to play two or three games a week. It was like a D league. The team that I played for was almost like a YMCA team. They could have one American player on the team. That American player would get paid, but everybody else on the team would not. The players all had jobs in the community. There were players who worked in construction and in plumbing. After work, they would come to practice or the game. The crowds were small, a mere 150 to 200 people a game.

"That's where I had fallen to at that point in time. But I was still getting paid about $600, maybe $800 a month plus expenses They had a car and interpreter for me, but the expense money really covered what it cost to live in Switzerland, a very expensive country. I played a few games for them and lasted sixty to ninety days.

"I got me a commercial advertising mattresses. In the commercial, I try to show people who hired me for the commercial how big their mattresses were. I would lay on the mattress. I was one of the biggest people in the country. You could walk around the city and see my picture.

"I found an area where I could get drugs. I still thought I could do drugs and somehow play. I tried working on my condition, but I was getting older. It was getting a lot harder to work my way back into shape than when I was younger. Outside of practice and playing one game a week, I didn't have much to do. I had a lot of time on my hands, so I would walk around the city.

"I'm starting to look for certain things, but I couldn't find them. By certain things I mean drug dealers. Finally, I located a place that had drugs. I went inside and saw that they have every kind of drug in the world. The only problem: you can't take them out.

"I would never ask for cocaine. I would always say, 'where can I find some weed?' And they would say, 'well, you have to go to such and such an area. That's where everything is at.' The only thing is—you had to consume the drug inside. That was okay for me. I didn't particularly like to consume drugs by myself. I thought it would be even better to do it inside because now I'm not doing drugs by myself.

"I ran across a kid over there by the name of Donnie McDade, a Black guy. He'd been over there for a while. He befriended me. He would come by my room, take me around and show me stuff. This was before I found a drug area.

"I got a chance to play against him. He was averaging thirty-eight or forty points a game, something like that. I was averaging almost eighteen points. When we played against each other he had, like, forty-six or forty-seven points. I believe I scored my average of eighteen points against him. I said to myself: 'How can I perform at an NBA standard or anything like that when this kid is scoring that many points against me.' At this point I was kind of tired. I lost a step. I'm depressed, which gave me a reason to get high."

Washburn spent about ninety days in Switzerland playing basketball before he was released. Washburn's team would not make the playoffs, so there was no need to keep him around. Jake Talley, Washburn's agent, was a little happier this time. Washburn had stuck out the assignment. Still, he was a little upset that he had not lost the weight he had promised to lose."

It was not too long after his return to the U.S. that he got another offer to play overseas. This time, it would be Puerto Rico.

CHRIS WASHBURN: "I don't know who set it up, but my mother got a call, and she told me I had an opportunity to go overseas again. It would be a short season, but I was willing to give it a try. Once I got there, however, it would turn out to be the same thing all over again."

The team Washburn played for was the Indios de Mayaguez. The city of Mayagüez is located in the center of the western coast on the island of Puerto Rico and has a population of a little over 73,000. The team plays in the Baloncesto Superior Nacional (BSN). He met with the coaches but did not get to see the team.

CHRIS WASHBURN: "I still wasn't in shape, but I went anyway. They put me up in a nice apartment. Soon after I got there, I'm doing drugs. I lost time because I'm getting high. I am doing drugs 'til daylight. Then someone from the team comes to get me. They knock, but I don't answer. They leave. A little while later, they come back and knock again.

I put a chair up against the door. I've lost track of time, and I'm coming down from the drugs I've taken.

"I still want more drugs, so I finally left the room. I met one of the team assistants. He asks me if I'm alright. I say, yeah. I tell him I fell asleep and lost track of time. I guess jet lag got me. Finally on the third day there, they told me they weren't gonna be able to use me. I was on a flight back to the States."

Washburn had five chances overseas to work his way back into pro basketball. He had flopped with every team. Most players, at this point in their career, would be devastated or desperate. Not Chris Washburn. He merely shrugged and continued to pursue his drug-induced lifestyle.

CHRIS WASHBURN: "Basketball at that time was just something where I could use my name to make some quick money. By the time they saw me play, I'd already have the money from them. Once overseas, my main goal was to find the drug spots. At that point in time, I wanted to do drugs more than anything. I was totally self-focused. Could somebody talk to me? Not really. I really didn't have anybody who I would have listened to. At that time, I didn't have the right influences around me."

When Washburn returned to Hickory after his latest venture abroad, he still went out into the streets to get high. Bam was one of Washburn's regular drug dealers in Hickory.

Bam recalls the time he got Washburn to kick another drug user in the chest. The user owed Bam money.

BAM: "The dude owed me money, but he wouldn't pay me. Chris and I were sitting in the projects when the dude came up. I got Chris to kick him in the chest, and he paid me.

"Chris was always in the street looking for drugs. He was seriously on crack. I would see him four five times a day walking the street."

Washburn's agent called him one day to say there were still teams overseas that were interested in him. 'Stand by and get yourself together.' Washburn was still willing to go overseas, but then he got shot in the foot in a parking lot in a part of Hickory known for drug activity.

CHRIS WASHBURN: "I had been doing drugs for a few days. I got the drugs from a friend of mine. I owed him some money. I told him I would come back later and pay him. I had just come back from overseas, so I had some money. One afternoon, my friend was with the guy that he gets his drugs from, the supplier. I was up the block, and they came by. They spotted me. His supplier told my friend to get that money from me. My friend approached me and asked for the money. I told him I didn't have it, but I said, 'I'll get it for you in the morning.' My friend said that the supplier wanted the money right now. So, the guy gave my friend a gun to shoot me.

"My friend didn't want to shoot me, but he's aiming towards my face and my chest. I grabbed a guy beside me, picked him up in a bear hug and held him in front of me. I kept moving, holding the guy in front of me, so he couldn't shoot me, but he shot me in the foot. I felt the foot burn. So, I dropped the guy and hobbled off.

"I hustled away on pure adrenaline down the hill to another friend's house and sat on the porch. The man in the house came out and asked me: 'Did you hear that gun shot?' I said, 'Yeah. I think I got shot.' I reached down to touch my foot, and I gently squeezed it. There was no blood. I took the shoe off, and my whole sock was full of blood.

"I thought I got shot with a BB gun because the hole was so small. But they told me that it was a 38 hollow. Eventually, they found out who it was. And then at that time, because I'm drug induced, I wanna try and go make the bond for my friend. I don't know how much it was, but I just wanted to do it."

"That was the second time someone had tried to shoot me. Prior to that, a few weeks earlier, a guy had walked up to me. I didn't owe him any money. He was just mad because I wouldn't buy drugs from him. He tried to shoot me. I took the gun from him and shot at him. I didn't hit him. I ended up keeping the gun and selling it for drugs.

"As for being shot in the foot, the bullet didn't really hurt me that badly. The doctor told me it wouldn't be good for me to try and jump and or put a lot of pressure on it because the way it damaged my bones and my foot, at any time, my foot could have just broken in half.

"Even to this day there's a big hole in my foot, down through the bone, and I have a lot of fragments still in there from the bullet. I still had an opportunity to go play somewhere, but the doctor told me there was no way that I could play. I couldn't put a lot of pressure on the foot. So, after I got shot, basketball was over for me."

Hickory police said Washburn gave authorities two different stories about the incident. First, Washburn said it was an accident. Then he told police he was shot by someone to whom he owed money. Washburn was not seriously injured, police told Charlotte television station WBTV. He was treated and released from a Hickory hospital. No one has ever been arrested in the case, police reveal. To this day, Chris Washburn walks with a limp.

11

STRUGGLE

"I was unreliable. My word wasn't good. I would tell her things that weren't true. She really didn't trust leaving the kids with me. But still she stuck with me for a long time." ~ Chris Washburn

After Washburn was shot, he could not do the only thing he knew how to do: play basketball. The foot wound had made it difficult for him to move like a pro basketball player should. Still, he took his situation in stride.

CHRIS WASHBURN: "I had a little money left from playing overseas, so we weren't destitute. I really didn't want to play because everywhere I went, I was being sent home. Now I have a reason not to go. I'd been shot."

In 1997, Washburn went to war with Hollywood, suing CBS and Warner Brothers for $20 million. He charged that the film Inaccurately depicted him as a drug addict. The film, "Never Give Up: The Jimmy V Story," depicts the life of Jim Valvano while he was a coach at NC State in the early to mid-1980s. The documentary was broadcast on April 2, 1986, on CBS. Valvano died in 1993. The film was directed by Marcus Cole and starred Anthony LaPaglia as Jim Valvano. In the papers filed by Washburn's attorney, Washburn charged that the depiction of him in the movie held him up to "disgrace and ridicule" and defamed his reputation.

CHRIS WASHBURN: "Someone had gotten in touch with me about the movie and urged that I should sue CBS and Warner Brothers. He put me in touch with a lawyer who was willing to take my case. The friend said I should have been compensated because others depicted in the movie were compensated. I wasn't compensated at all for that movie, and no one from CBS or Warner contacted me. In the movie, they had my last name on the back of an actor's basketball jersey and the character supposedly arrived at NC State in 1983, the time I was actually in high school."

Washburn said he was denied reinstatement to the NBA shortly after the movie aired "on April 2, 1986. Scott D. Pierce, a television reporter for the *Deseret News,* wrote in the newspaper on April 2, 1996, that the film has plenty of problems, including "a dozen jumps in time period, some truly awful editing of footage of the fictional Valvano (Anthony LaPaglia) and his fictional team with actual videotape of the Wolfpack winning the title, and a tendency toward TV cliches."

CHRIS WASHBURN: "The lawyer who worked the case was about ready to sue when he passed away. Someone in his office took over his cases, but they dropped the ball. They didn't go to court to represent me on the case within the allotted time and, it was dismissed. So, I let the matter go and went on to other things."

The case was still ongoing the following year when Washburn had a more pleasant experience. He was invited back to NC State after an absence of twelve years. The crowd at Reynolds Auditorium buzzed when Washburn took the court for the alumni game, which included other ex-Wolfpack players, including Vann Williford, George Smedes York, and Rick Anheuser. The press reported one fan commenting, "I can't believe Chris Washburn came back. It's really strange seeing him out there after all that went on."

CHRIS WASHBURN: "I was a little nervous coming back after all those years, but I was treated with respect. They invited all the players to come back. A lot of us got to play in the game. Now, a few years prior to that, when I was still actively using drugs, I went down and got to play in a game involving the current team against the veterans. They beat our butt, but I was out there.

"This time, I had to sit on the bench because of the bullet that injured my leg. I wouldn't expect a bad reception at NC State because, although I made some freshman mistakes, I went out and I played hard. I left everything on the court at that time. So, I think folks remember me from that part."

Washburn says he felt ignored in the North Carolina community, conceding that his troubles have cost him recognition. He noticed that he wasn't mentioned as one of Hickory's famous athletes on the city's Wikipedia page.

No matter how bad his life seemed, Washburn tried to remain upbeat. But there was one time when he thought about ending it all.

CHRIS WASHBURN: "I remember when things weren't going well. That was when I ended up in jail a lot. I had got my hands on a gun, and I was gonna sell it to get some money for drugs. I pulled the trigger back on the gun, a 357. I didn't want to shoot myself in the face. I thought about shooting myself in the chest. Then I remembered that the guy who supplied me with drugs was out of town, but he had said to me that when he came back to town, he had some drugs that he wanted me to test for him. I said to myself: 'Well, I can't let him down. So, I won't kill myself today.' That was the only suicide thought I ever had. Cocaine saved me at that point in time because I knew a friend of mine who had some drugs for me that he wanted me to try."

By the mid-1990s, life for Washburn had become a daily struggle. He was almost out of money, and someone had to make it for the Washburn family to survive. That someone would be Chris Washburn's wife, Michelle. She had once worked in an office and had been a manager for Sprint while living in New York City. Now, she would work at anything she could find.

Michelle found work in a factory. It was hard work. Washburn remembers Michelle coming home covered in oil and dirt.

CHRIS WASHBURN: "She worked at something totally different than what she was accustomed to, but she did it. We were living with my mom and dad, but we needed to have some income coming in. I had to use crutches, but I was still going out on the street and getting high. My wife would be riding with the kids in the car, and they would see me and wave. I'll be on crutches trying to get high."

Washburn had been with Michelle since he got stuck in Philadelphia, Mississippi, and she had sent him a bus ticket so he could make it to Dallas, Texas.

CHRIS WASHBURN: "I arrived with only one bag. Michelle took me to her family house because she was staying there. Her mom and dad were separated. Her dad was living in another part of Texas. Her mom was living not far from the family house."

At first, Chris and Michelle got along well, but then problems started to arise.

CHRIS WASHBURN: "I was unreliable. My word wasn't good. I would tell her things that weren't true. She really didn't trust leaving the kids with me. But still she stuck with me for a long time. We met in '86, but we were together about twelve years before we got married. Michelle didn't want to have another kid out of wedlock. Eventually she left me. She was tired of the lifestyle I was living. I can remember sitting all alone in the apartment crying. She gave me plenty of time to get myself right, but I couldn't, I wouldn't. I spent all those years with her but couldn't change."

In 1994, Washburn received the court's decision on his appeal to the 1991 conviction on drug possession. His appeal was denied, and he would begin serving three years for the conviction.

CHRIS WASHBURN: "My past had caught up with me, and I had a debt I had to pay. I was sent to a place they called the John M. Wynne Unit, located in Huntsville, Texas, a little over an hour's drive from Houston. My wife took my reincarceration pretty good. She was tired of me running the streets, looking for drugs. With me being in prison, she at least knew where I was, and maybe I would have the opportunity of getting straight.

"But prison turned out to almost like being on the streets. It didn't have all the things you find in civilian life, but one of the things it did have were plenty of drugs. I was in prison with some of the top drug dealers in the country. They had homeboys who served as bodyguards for them. Drugs were freaking coming into the prison!

"I got high on crack one time in prison. It made me so paranoid and nervous. I was excited to smoke crack, but once I did it, I started getting paranoid, looking around for police. I wouldn't leave my cell. I could have had more access to crack, but I ended up smoking marijuana. Now I'm in prison, but the same thing is starting to happen to me. I'm starting to get involved with drugs. That's not, you know, what prison is about.

"Prison life was kind of lonely. Out of 4,000 or 5,000 inmates I was the only guy from North Carolina. But the inmates knew who I was and that gave me some notoriety. That and the fact that I was huge guy meant nobody messed with me. A lot of guys in there were basketball enthusiasts. I mean they played street ball or basketball in high school, and some of them did it in college. As for the guards, some were good, some were bad. Some of the guards were former athletes who never really had the next level gear to go higher.

"They played in high school or a little college ball but dreamed of going higher. So, when a guard sees a guy enter that prison with all the ability in the world and throws it away, they weren't too sympathetic."

Washburn played basketball for the prison team. He describes the experience as depressing.

CHRIS WASHBURN: "I had played in the NBA where the hardwood floors are polished. I could look up in the stands and see thousands of people looking on. Now I'm on a prison bench. The guy beside me has on army boots. Another guy has flip flops taped to his feet. We're playing on concrete. There are six cheerleaders, all of them men. They all got lipstick on and are trying to move like an LA Lakers cheerleader. I was coming off the bench, not even starting at the damn penitentiary.

"After the game, I would go to my cell and lay down. I'd think: Just a few years ago, I was in the NBA. Now I have fallen to this point."

Washburn played basketball in prison with John Drew, another noted basketball player. Drew was a small forward from Gardner–Webb University who played eleven seasons in the NBA. Drew was a two-time NBA All-Star and was the first player banned under the substance abuse policy instituted by league commissioner David Stern.

CHRIS WASHBURN: "The prison kept us busy. I was up at 6 in the morning to go out into the field and do roadwork, cut the grass, dig ditches and things like that. They didn't have any boots my size in stock in my size. So, for almost the first six or seven months, I didn't work because they didn't have any shoes that fit me. All I had were tennis shoes, and I couldn't do that kind of work with just tennis shoes on. But eventually, they got me some boots I could wear.

"I was imprisoned far away from Michelle. She did come to visit me twice. The first time she came by herself. The second time she brought the kids. I really didn't want her to come.

"I spent about ten or eleven months in prison that time, then got out on parole. There were some stipulations about my release. One of them was that I couldn't leave the state of Texas without permission from the court. Then the opportunity to play in Switzerland came up. So, I took it. I was in Switzerland about three to four months. During that time, I missed my parole visits, so I would have a violation when I came back to Texas or anywhere in United States. I was getting high and not thinking about my parole violation when I got picked up. This time I would have to spend fourteen months in prison. They sent me to a place called Goree prison. From there to the T. L Roach Unit in Childress, Texas.

"Then I was sent to a prison in Arkansas. Talk about it being cold. I think they sent me there mainly because they were spiteful about the cigarette thing. It wasn't a big unit. It contained about 200 inmates."

Finally, Chris Washburn got out of prison. Relations with Michelle had cooled, and they were not communicating. Washburn thought his wife was in Houston, but she had moved to Dallas. He followed her to Dallas. On top of that, Washburn's father was not doing well healthwise, and the couple moved to Hickory to keep an eye on him.

People in Hickory had not seen Chris in a couple of years. They would ask Chris, 'where have you been playing ball?' Washburn would tell them: overseas. Washburn's money had run out, and he got a job in security. But he could not stay away from the drug scene, and he was back on the streets looking for his next high.

Washburn's father had been battling prostate cancer for years, but now his condition had deteriorated.

CHRIS WASHBURN: "My father's cancer had gone into remission, but he was getting older, and the cancer came back more aggressively. I wasn't going out in the streets as much because I was concerned about him. My mom was always a strong person. Even at the funeral she was stern and firm as she had always been. I was the only one crying.

"The last day (of my father's life) was kinda hard. He didn't want to go to a nursing home. I was worrying about my mother. If my father passed, I would be the only one she had. I decided I would stop using drugs. And just like that I quit.

"In the last days, I would have to carry him downstairs because he was too weak to walk. I would sit him on the couch and prop him up. Then at night I'd bring him back upstairs. On his last day, I went to the store. When I came back home, my mom said: 'Your father is dead.'"

Washburn admits that he viewed his father's death as a way of gaining sympathy on the street so he could get free drugs or the money to buy them.

CHRIS WASHBURN: "Being from a small community, everybody knew my father had passed. Even the drug dealers were sympathetic. I got free drugs because of that. But I knew my drug use was not gonna last much longer, even though I knew it would be hard to quit. At least I had moved in the right direction. I had accepted the fact that I was addicted. When I accepted that fact, drugs stopped being fun to use."

It would be challenging to quit cold turkey, though, because Washburn's drug use had helped support the drug trafficking community. He was spending $400 to $500 a day on drugs. Sometimes, he would drive the drug dealers who didn't have cars around town in return for drugs. Sometimes he would rent his car out.

So slowly but surely, Washburn began weaning his way off of drugs. Washburn decided not to seek help. He had gone that route before without success. He felt his way to recovery was to wean his way off the selfish mindset drug addicts have. The universe revolves around them, or so the drug dealers thought. Once he was finally free of drug addiction, Washburn decided he would share his story with the world in the hope he could help others.

Weaning his way off of drug addiction came at a time when his marriage was in trouble. Michelle had stuck with her husband with his serious drug addiction since the mid-1980s, and she was tired that her husband's problem never seemed to have an end.

CHRIS WASHBURN: "After my father passed, I was really trying to make our marriage work. We had been together all those years and Michelle was tired of me trying to get it right, even though now I was really trying. I wanted her to forget about our past and work for the future, but she didn't want to do that. She simply didn't trust me to do the right thing. So, my thing was, well, if you don't want me to be the chief of this tribe, I'll go somewhere else to start my own tribe. So, I left and got my first apartment."

Chris and Michelle eventually got back together, and after three years in Hickory, they moved back to Dallas. But once again they separated.

Washburn met Dee J. (not her real name) about a month after he had separated from Michelle. Today, Dee is an embalmer at her uncle's funeral home in Dallas, Texas. In 2000, Dee worked in the credit department of a company named Diamond Chrysler Collections. Dee recalls how she met Chris.

DEE J.: "It was at a pool hall. Chris was going to meet a young lady with whom I worked. She was having car issues, and I had been transporting her around. She asked if I would be interested in taking her to go meet this guy. I told her no. But then she said would I be so kind as to have a drink with her because she had finally got her car fixed and wanted to celebrate. I said, 'Okay. Cool. Let's go have a drink.'"

CHRIS WASHBURN: "I was working security. I'm walking around the club, flirting and talking with everybody. I knew Dee's girlfriend liked me, but she had a cocked eye, you know, one of her eyes wasn't straight. It went off to the right. I didn't really like that."

DEE J: "We went to the bar, and Chris was there. We sat down and my friend started talking with Chris. I was sitting there enjoying my drink. I really didn't pay Chris any attention. They eventually left the pool hall together, but before my friend did, she asked for one of my business cards. She put her phone number on that card. She told Chris that if he couldn't get in touch with her, he was to call the number on the business card, which was my number.

"He ended up calling me. I saw my girlfriend a few days later and asked if Chris had called her. She said, 'no' Then he called me again, and I asked if he wanted to talk to my girlfriend. He said: 'No. I want to talk to you.' So, I started going out with him.

"What's funny was my girlfriend was telling everyone at work (we worked together) that she was going out with Chris. He was taking her here. He was taking her there. They were doing this and that. And I'm thinking, What? It's all fiction. Chris said, 'why don't you just tell her?' I never did. She ended up getting let go from the job.

"My relationship with Chris would last ten years. I didn't know who Chris was when I met him. But playing basketball made sense given his height. What was fun about our relationship was that he didn't have to live like any type of persona or name, or it wasn't important who he was or how he had to be or who people thought he was and how they thought he should be. It was just about enjoying Chris for being Chris. And he was a lot of fun."

When Dee met Chris, she found him to be a "great stand-up guy" who did not show any signs around her of having a drug problem.

DEE J: "I met a guy who had found himself, who knew what he was doing and who he was. He was very aware of where he wanted to go and what he wanted to do. And I got the opportunity to hang out with the guy, the man, not the persona, not the ball player, not the ego, not any of that. Because even with our relationship, he was humble enough to say, you know what? I'm gonna go to work, and I'm gonna do what I have to do."

"We had great times. I'd wake up in the middle of night, pick him up, and we'd go somewhere, get something to eat, talk. We loved this Chinese restaurant that stayed open until 4 am. We'd sit there, eat and talk, not thinking about the time."

Then one day Dee helped stop Chris from being robbed. Chris had given her a key to his apartment, and she had gone over when Chris was at work to use the gym in the complex. Three men were in the house. Two of them were in the hallway, and another was in the back bedroom.

DEE J: "They had some things in their hands. I rushed downstairs, got in my car, and called Chris. Chris came to the house. When he got there, I told him everything, the three guys were gone. He could see things were in disarray, I was lucky that nothing bad happened to me. No one was ever charged."

Although Washburn was seeing Dee, he moved back in with Michelle. He had not been with Michelle for some time but was still comfortable with her.

CHRIS WASHBURN: "Dee would meet me at the at the pool hall where I was working, and then she would drop me off around the corner from my house and then I would go home with Michelle. But after a while, Michelle caught on. And so now it's time for me to make my decision."

Things at home weren't getting any better, and Michelle was on to her husband's relationship with Dee.

Michelle had even confronted Dee about it.

DEE J. "Michelle would come by my place and case out the house. One time we got into it, and I was like, 'you can tell her to come pick you up.' We argued and he left. Later on, we ended up getting back together."

On another occasion, Dee was at Washburn's place working out in the gym.

Dee J: "Michelle came over to the apartment complex and keyed my car. Keyed my whole damn car! We got into it. Chris happened to have been out of town. He was visiting his mom at the time. And I called him and told him what happened.

"He called Michelle and told her: 'you are out of line. You are wrong. You need to get yourself together.'"

CHRIS WASHBURN: "Police were called. Michelle had to end up paying a lot of money. Then I got calls. Dee called me and explained the situation and how they had gotten into a fight. And then I got a call from Michelle explaining how she saw the situation. My wife wanted me to tell Dee not to press charges, but they ended up going to court. My wife had to pay some money for the damage that she had done to Dee's car.

"I think that was when Michelle figured out we wouldn't be getting back together. But, again, I'd always still try to maintain some kind of relationship with Michelle because we still had two kids together."

One day, Washburn asked Dee what she did at her job. Dee explained that her job was making people feel comfortable so that they would want to pay their bills. Chris said, "Okay, I can do that." Dee told him that some jobs at her company were opening up. She would check it out and get back to him. She returned to tell Chris her company was indeed hiring. Dee had Chris compile a resume and even got him an interview.

CHRIS WASHBURN: "I got the job. It seemed the people who were hiring actually knew who I was. I think being ex-NBA helped get me the job. After a training period, I went to work. Now the strange thing was I didn't know how to type. So, every time I typed I had to look at the keys. I was a little slow. My coworkers saw that I didn't know how to type and decided to play a joke on me. On break one day, they changed the lettering on the typewriter keys. So. when I came back and started typing, say for example, an "A," there would be a "U" there instead. The words did not make sense, but a co-worker came to my aid and changed the lettering on the keys from what they were.

"I started to fit in. I stayed at that job for about two years. The only bad thing about the job was that it was low paying… about $13 an hour, but jobs were becoming available, and I had experience. So, I started applying for other positions, then another company came along by the name of Triad Financial. They were offering anywhere between $17 to $20 an hour. Now, again, I still didn't have a lot of experience, but I applied anyway and got the job. It helped, I think, that the company was out in California and that I had played with Golden State. They knew my name."

"When I got there, I was doing the exact same thing and now I'm getting paid $18 an hour. They had contests to encourage their collectors. One of the contests involved answering the question: how much money can you collect within a month's time? The company record was like $98,000 for one collector. I broke the record. Before I left, I collected more money in a one-month period than anybody in the company's history, about $110,000. Then I got fired shortly after I had a new manager. I felt I knew more than a manager did, but you know authority.

"I continued to work in collections, but then I got a call. I had to go home because my mother had dementia, and she couldn't take care of herself."

Meanwhile, Washburn's relationship with Dee had lasted ten years, but one day, Dee J. knew it had to end.

DEE J: "I wanted to take our relationship to the next level. I was in a relationship with Chris for a long time, but I wanted to get married. I was ready to get married. I knew what I wanted to do. But Chris was just finding himself. He wasn't ready to make the move. It was hard, but we broke up, I wanted to get married, and eventually I did."

Washburn was torn between two women. Each of them provided him with something he needed in his life. But he also knew he had to end his relationship with Dee.

Meanwhile, Chris's friendship with Michelle was improving. They had become cordial with each other. Michelle had accepted the fact that they would probably not get back together but that they should get along for the sake of the kids. Then another tragedy struck.

CHRIS WASHBURN: "Me and Michelle started getting along. We started talking to each other again. The bitterness in our friendship was gone. She stopped listening to the people that were saying bad things about me and started looking at my actual actions and how I was staying clean. She called me and told me that Chris, our son, was getting ready to go to UTEP for a visit and to see if he wanted to go to school there. I told her call me when he gets back. I wanted to see how it went.

"So, it was a normal weekend when I got a call from our son, Darius. The call was on Michelle's phone. He says Mama died. I said, 'What do you mean Mama died?' He said Michelle was in the bathroom, fell and hit her head. I was in complete shock. I tried calling to talk to the kids, but nobody let me through because they don't know that we've patched up our differences. They're still treating me like a bad person. A pariah. But I'm still married to her, although we are separated, and I still had a lot of say in what was going to be done even with her body.

"I went to Texas for the funeral. I don't know what the problem was. At Michelle's funeral, I forced my way to the front row, but I was made to sit in the back row. I got into it with Michelle's family. Her mother said I didn't even pay for this funeral. So, I pulled out a stack of money from my pocket to show her I could have paid for the funeral. I just didn't know about it. It was a real mess. I ended up having to leave the funeral.

"I came back to North Carolina, and the kids stayed with the grandma, Michelle's mother. I had to deal with her death mostly by myself. I had been with her for thirteen years. That really hurt."

12

REDEMPTION

"I had a few drinks, and I was feeling pretty good, cocky, in fact. I clicked on my cell phone and showed her a picture of me in the NBA. I didn't tell her I had been banned from the NBA. She didn't know who I was, and she didn't seem to care about me having played in the NBA." ~ Chris Washburn

Around 2010, Washburn began to worry that his mother had Alzheimer's disease. He was still living in Dallas, but, in his phone calls with his mom, Washburn suspected something was not right. He saw signs in their conversations that she was slipping mentally.

Relatives would call Washburn, concerned. They would tell him mom had a hard time remembering where she had put her car keys. She had stopped at a stop light once and became confused about what her next move should be. Fortunately, she recovered, drove on, and no one had been hurt. His mother's license was about to expire, and they wondered if they should help get it renewed.

His mother had given one of her cousins power of attorney, but then Chris found out that the cousin had taken advantage of his mother and had stolen $60,000 to $70,000 from her. The theft destroyed his mother's finances and nearly bankrupted her, and she was about thirty to forty-five days from being put out of the house that her son had bought for her with his Golden State signing money in 1986.

Washburn had more than his mother to worry about. He was having problems with Dee, his girlfriend of ten years. Chris and Dee were simply not seeing things eye to eye. But then, in 2009, he met Monique Richardson in a bar. Monique was with friends, trying to reduce the stress from a tough day at work and having to deal with her kids.

MONIQUE WASHBURN: "My children didn't do their chores one night when I got home from work. I was tired and stressed, so I called my girlfriend and said we needed to go out and have a couple of drinks. We went to a sports bar, and Chris walked in. It's been pretty much us against the world ever since.

"When he walked in, I tapped one of my girlfriends and said: 'Look.' He was big. He had to duck under the doorway. He looked around, and we locked eyes. He walked directly up to me and asked me where my man was. I told him I didn't have one. And then he said, 'Bring your ass over here to VIP.' He left and sat down, expecting me to come over. I looked at my girlfriend and said, 'Who the hell does he think he's talking to?'

"So, I stayed where I was. He sent a friend over to tell me to join him in VIP. I sent him back with the message: I was with my girlfriends, and I wasn't going to come over. He came back and said he is really persistent. So we finally went over.

"The first thing he did was take his phone out and show me some photos of him playing basketball. He said, 'Look. I'm Chris Washburn.' I kinda pushed his phone away and said, 'That was back in the eighties. Who are you now?' He laughed. So, we talked a little bit and that started our relationship."

Chris Washburn remembers the meeting.

CHRIS WASHBURN: "I had a few drinks, and I was feeling pretty good, cocky, in fact. I clicked on my cell phone and showed her a picture of me in the NBA. I didn't tell her I had been banned from the league. She didn't know who I was, and she didn't seem to care about me having played in the NBA."

MONIQUE WASHBURN "He told me he was going through an ugly breakup at the time, and I was like, okay. So long as you are not together now, it's fine. I wasn't really big into sports, although I did like football. But I didn't follow basketball, so I didn't know who he was or know about his history. I didn't find all of that out until sometime into our relationship when he started telling me more about himself."

Their relationship got off to a rocky start. Washburn was separated from Dee, but Monique still had to deal with it. She didn't want to get in the middle of their separation. She didn't want any drama in her life. She talked with her roommate, who told her that Chris was going through a bad breakup and advised her to give him a chance. So, she did.

Monique eventually began to learn about Washburn's past.

MONIQUE WASHBURN: "Before Chris, I was married to a crackhead, the father of my children, so I knew about drug addiction. I told Chris when he told me about his past that, so long as that's not who you are now, we can move forward. So, I knew the signs of drug addiction and when somebody was using, and Chris has not used since we had been together.

"Chris has taken responsibility for his life. When somebody has that true desire to stop, they can stop, but it has to be from their heart. It can't be, 'I'm gonna stop using because of this person or that person, or this rehab or that rehab.' Generally, when people do stop using, it's because they had some type of epiphany telling them that they can't keep doing drugs anymore."

In January 2011, Monique persuaded Chris that they should open a restaurant in Hickory. Chris received an insurance payment of $100,000 from the NBA, and they still hadn't spent much of that money.

CHRIS WASHBURN: "Monique always wanted to cook and to have her own restaurant. One of the restaurants on my side of town where I was raised came open. It needed a little work that would cost me about $40,000 to get the building up to code. I also had to buy equipment. But toward the end of getting the building in shape, I almost ran out of money. I didn't even have enough money to buy food. I had to try to borrow money and go to the pawn shop.

"During that time, I was working on my credit because my credit score was shot. Up until opening that restaurant, I didn't need anything on credit. But I was getting older, and I started to see that I needed to have a good credit score. I started working on that. I could get loans just off of my credit, and that made me feel good because now people are starting to trust me again. Banks are calling me, wanting to give me money. And that's how the restaurant got started."

The house recipes like fried chicken and pork chops came from Monique.

CHRIS WASHBURN (joking): "I can only take credit for the potatoes, cold slaw, and chicken salad."

Chris and Monique kept the prices below $5 for most dishes. They allowed customers who were broke but hungry, and Washburn and Monique had them work for their food. Monique's children, Montavia and Davon, helped out behind the counter. Davon even designed the menu.

The restaurant lasted for two and a half years. Near the end, Chris hired a lot of employees who were friends.

CHRIS WASHBURN: "We were making money, but as they say, a business is only as good as the people who work for it. We had good employees to start with, but we were running a fast-food place, so there was a lot of turn over. It was actually hard to find people who wanted to work.

"People would not show up for work. I hired a lot of friends, and they took our friendship for granted. We were counting on them to show up, and when it was time for their shift, they wouldn't come in. This was especially true on the weekends. They'd get drunk, and when I called and asked them what happened, they would say they didn't feel too good and won't be becoming in."

The restaurant closed. A little while later, Washburn found himself once again in legal trouble. In early June 2014, he was arrested for obtaining property by false pretense. The incident occurred at a Q-Express gas station. Washburn was driving a white SUV that pulled up to a gas pump at the express, which was located at 525 Fourth St. SW in Hickory.

Michael Izard, the passenger in the car, was also arrested for obtaining property by false pretense. Izard tried to pay for the fuel with a WEX/Fleet Fuel card, but the card was denied. Izard told the manager he would come back and pay for the gas. Izard was given a $5,000 unsecured bond, according to his arrest report.

The cashier activated the pump, and Washburn filled the gas tank, which cost about $56, before driving to the front of the store to pick up Izard. As Izard climbed into the van, Washburn asked, "Is everything okay?" He said, "Yes." Washburn gave Izard $25 and promised to give him the remaining $3 the next time he saw Izard. Washburn then dropped Izard off at their friend's house.

Izard was arrested on May 28 on charges of felony obtaining property by false pretense and misdemeanor possession of stolen property. Police showed up at Washburn's home June 6 to arrest him.

"I honestly didn't know what the officer was talking about until I got my papers and saw (Izard's) name on there," Washburn said. "I didn't know I was doing anything wrong."

Monique and Chris had been together two years when they moved to Hickory in 2011 to take care of Chris's mother. Monique made it clear to Chris that she was giving up her entire life to come with him to take care of his mother, and she hoped that soon they would get married. The uncertainty was gnawing at their relationship, and Monique decided It was time to split with Chris.

MONIQUE WASHBURN: "Up to 2016, there was still no proposal, no move towards marriage. I'm taking full-time care of his mom, his house, doing everything that a wife's supposed to do. I'm also dealing with other females of his on a regular basis. We were constantly arguing about the disrespect that I was being given.

"So, in 2017 I took my daughter, moved out of his house, and got my own place in Hickory. He had another girlfriend less than 30 days later. She was one of the girls that we had been arguing about. So, I moved on and allowed him to have his relationship with her.

"About a year and a half of Chris dating her, I started dating somebody. Mind you, through that whole period, he was still doing everything he could to hold on to me. I would get flowers and gifts at work. He would call me constantly."

Then the pandemic happened, and that's when Chris decided he needed to break up with his girlfriend and make amends with Monique.

In 2020, Washburn's mother had a stroke. She was not responding well to treatment. Washburn called Monique and asked her if she could come over. Monique took Washburn's mother to the hospital. Monique wound up spending every day staying at the house and helping out with his mom. Meanwhile, she had several discussions with Chris; they decided that he was going to stop seeing the new girlfriend, and Monique would stop seeing her boyfriend. They would give their relationship a second chance.

Just before they got back together, his mom died on May 15, 2020. She was 91.

In August 2020, Monique was coming out of a shower, naked, about to get dressed for work. Washburn was sitting on the corner of the bed. He had a ring in his hand. Chris asked Monique for her hand in marriage. They got married on April 23, 2022.

MONIQUE WASHBURN: "Chris later explained to me that he had been trying to work up the nerve to propose. He is a much better husband than he was a boyfriend. I don't have the problems with all the females anymore. He's very respectful in that manner, as far as I know."

"Something clicked with him when we got married in the way he protects me, the way he talks to me, the way he handles me. Something has completely shifted in him. I tell people all the time. We are closer than we have ever been."

CHRIS WASHBURN: "I had to throw the towel in. I was too old to cast my line back out there to see what I was gonna get. I was happy with Monique. She had done everything I needed her to do. Monique put a lot of work into me. I just feel obligated to make our relationship work.

"Besides, she was starting to get weird on me. At that time, I was overweight. I was about 430, 440 pounds. I could drop dead at any moment. I wasn't in really good health. Monique said that if I died, she could be thrown out of our house. So she was like anything happened to you right now, your kids come and take the house and I'd be on the streets. And I can understand that. She needed some stability in her life. I had to not just look out for me. I had to look out for her and her daughter. That's when I married her."

As Washburn got older, he began to think more often about his ancestry. He knew he was adopted but knew nothing about his roots. As he got older, the question of where he came from became more pressing. He needed answers. So, when he was about forty-seven years old, Washburn approached his biological mother.

CHRIS WASHBURN: "I was going to the doctor, and he kept asking me about my family history. I was getting embarrassed because I couldn't provide answers. I remember my mom telling me that if I ever wanted to find out anything about my background. There was a file at Social Services. And I don't know why that popped in my mind then, I guess because my mom had dementia and was getting older, and I was afraid she might not remember or help me much to find out who I am.

"I filled out the information and sent it in. About a month or so went by, and I got a response from Social Services. They wanted me to come in. I went down and spoke to a lady. She told me that they had found my biological mother. If she wanted to see me, she would get in contact with me.

"They didn't want to give me the contact information for my mother because a lot of times people get upset because they expect anonymity. So, I had to reassure them that I just wanted to know where I came from. I'd heard stories over the years. Some of them weird. For instance, I might be one of my uncle's kids.

"So, Miss Ruby McClendon, my biological mother, called and told me who she was. I told her I would come to see her. I did. It was amazing. The mom who raised me had never had a drink or smoked. My biological mother, I found out, had never drank or smoked. Both were great cooks. My adopted mother made great pies, and my biological mom made great cakes. So, there was a lot of resemblance between them. And as for the husbands... My mom had married a man who liked alcohol, and my biological mom's husband liked alcohol as well. And so, the households were very similar.

"I met my brother, who was raised just like me as an only child. But at that time, I still hadn't met my father. Miss Ruby hadn't said anything about him. It would be almost five years before she started providing details. She didn't know how to get in touch with him, but I found out that he lived less than five miles away from my biological mother.

"I eventually met him a few years later. His name was Cornelius. He had one child beside me, a daughter. We all were addicted to crack at one point in time in our lives. I think I have a gene of addiction. I had told my children that they shouldn't try drugs because they had that gene of addiction and that came from me.

"Drugs were not the only thing I was addicted to. Years ago, I was on this apple kick. I was eating so many of them, that I got gout, and I had to quit. I still overdo it on some things, but they are not costing me thousands of dollars as cocaine did. Cocaine triggered that thing in my brain where I could never get enough."

Washburn has been eager to share his story with the public. He thought that perhaps going public with his story could help someone from going down the wrong road as he had done. In 2008 Washburn began his speaking career in Dallas.

CHRIS WASHBURN: "I was in downtown Dallas at a taco truck, and one of the guys at the truck asked me what I was doing. I told him collections. He said he was working close by at a rehab center, which was more like a men's halfway house. And so, he asked me to come over. I went there and met the guy who was actually running the meeting. He asked me, 'Would you like to come down and share your story.' I thought about it and said, 'Hey, no problem.'

"I came back the next weekend to tell my story. As I talked, I got emotional and cried a little bit. I saw other men cry as well because they had been doing some of the same things I had been doing. I thought I might be on to something. I liked talking. I saw a chance to get my story out. So that's when I started public speaking.

"People found out about me and asked me to come and speak. I started speaking to basketball teams, youth groups and churches. I spoke at a rehab center called Malachi House in Greensboro, North Carolina. They wanted me to come back and speak. By that time, I had a lot of experience speaking in public under my belt.

"Then my public speaking started to take off. Al Wood, a former North Carolina basketball player, got in touch with me, and I started doing speeches for him. My name started to get around after that. The funny thing was that the NBA asked me to come back and speak at what we call the RTP, that's the Rookie Transition Program. They didn't have that when I was coming into the league. It definitely would have helped me. It could have made me more aware of my surroundings and not be so quick to invite people into my circle.

"I ended speaking for the program. I was joined by some other players who had been through some of the same struggles as me. Then I started going to the so called Top 100 basketball camp, which was funded through the NBA. They are the top 100 high school players in the country… McDonald's All Americans. I worked with the kids. I did that for a couple of years.

"I got my certification through the top 100 program. Now I can even go back and coach in the NBA. Can't do college, though, because I don't have a degree. The NBA started coming back around a little bit, and I started to improve my relationship with the NBA. The NBA had never changed. I did. I actually now began to see what I had given up.

"I didn't have a lot of training in my speaking role. On stage I had to try different things. At first, I was all over the place. I had to get used to holding the microphone."

Then Washburn met GL Henderson, and he was put on a different platform. Henderson, a podcast host who builds himself as the "King of Relationship Drama." He was in drug and alcohol management program while in the army. Today, Henderson is the owner of Federal Drug Testing Services.

GL HENDERSON: "When I first met Chris in 2011, I was in the army as a recruiter trainer stationed at Fort Jackson,

South Carolina. I was close to retirement at that time. I used to go to Charlotte, North Carolina, because I have friends there. One night, I went to a club in the uptown area. I was with an old-school hip-hop artist, Dana Dane. We were going to see Curtis Blow perform.

"It just so happened that Chris was there at the event that night, and he came over to meet Dana Dane. We all were just sitting around talking, and Chris was talking about who he was. Then he found out that I had written a book, called *The Fantasy Master* and that I had my own radio show.

"Chris knew that Dana Dane had just written a book that he was trying to get going, and I was helping him promote it. So that's how we kinda got started.

"Then I got a call from Chris. 'Remember me? I met you in the club.' And I was like, 'Oh, okay. Cool, man.' And he said that he was serious about telling his story. So, I told him to come on down to Charlotte. I met him at my best friend's house."

"We sat down and he told me his story. He really has a story. I realized that we should probably stop talking. It was so much. It was like eating fine chocolate. You just need to eat one piece at a time, rather than gobbling it down in huge chunks, or you will get sick. It got to a point where I said: 'I can help you, but you have to be committed.' But Chris wasn't ready to commit. He had a lot still going on in his life. He had just got back with Monique, and he was just getting situated. His adopted mom was getting up in age and needed care.

"I didn't think that he had the time to commit to what needed to happen to try to get his story out. But I ended up working with him, and he ended up speaking at a lot of meetings."

Henderson says that the progress Washburn has made in dealing with his drug addiction has been commendable, given with what he has had to deal.

GL HENDERSON: "In talking with Chris, I can see he has the maturity now to deal with his addiction. He's dealt with a lot of adversity. I mean, you know, mother's Alzheimer's, father's death, trouble with the law, his split with Monique there for a while, and his failed business. Those were all issues that he has dealt with successfully. But he seems to have survived all of it, while not reverting back to his old lifestyle. I give him a lot of credit for that."

Henderson adds, however, that Washburn is not out of the woods yet. In fact, he may never be.

GL HENDERSON: "Chris will be tested, and we will see if he'll stay sober. If the opportunity presents itself again, will he be ready to resist? You know that people will continue to come out of the woodwork, and the drug dealers will continue to try him."

Chris Washburn has emerged from the depths of drug addiction and a controversial academic career that left him ill-suited for life after basketball. He has accepted the fact that he must live with the label of being one of the biggest drug busts in history. He has survived living as a homeless person, eating out of garbage cans, spending three years in jail, and being shot over a petty drug deal. He is proud of himself and the fact that he essentially decided on his own without entering a rehab program that he would get off of drugs.

As Washburn approaches age sixty, he is feeling pretty good about himself and the life he is living. Washburn has four children of his own and has adopted two with Monique. He feels that he is closer to his children than he has ever been.

The children say they don't have any hard feelings towards their father, given the life he has led.

Two of his children have played pro ball like their father. Washburn's third son, Julian Washburn, played for the University of Texas El Paso (UTEP), later becoming a professional basketball player. Washburn's younger son, Chris Washburn Jr., also played basketball for UTEP before transferring to Texas Christian University (TCU) in 2013. He was drafted by the Suns. His other son, Chris Lightner, signed a contract with the Harlem Globe Trotters.

CHRIS WASHBURN, Jr.: "We don't talk much, but we do get along. I always looked at my father as a free-spirited man who followed his own path. He is very charismatic, even with that gap in his teeth."

Chris Lightner, Washburn's son with former girlfriend Claire Lightner, describes his relationship with his father today as good and says he talks with him frequently.

CHRIS LIGHTNER: "Given what he's gone through, it is amazing he is alive. Yeah, he could have done things better, but his experience has taught me about life. You need to play out the hand you're dealt with."

Chris Lightner's mother, Claire, is friends with Chris Washburn to this day.

CLAIRE LIGHTNER: "It's quite remarkable how Chris quit drugs, how well he's doing today. He did it alone without any real help. He had tried therapy in the pros, but it didn't work."

Montavia Washburn, his stepdaughter through Monique, says she and her stepdad were always butting heads when she was a teenager.

MONTAVIA WASHBURN: "Like every teenage girl, I definitely went through a phase where I was not trying to hear anything my dad had to say, especially because he wasn't my birth father. I kinda felt like he tried to raise us in a way that reflected his time in military school. He was pretty strict back then, and as a teenage girl, I did not like that. But as I got older, I started to change. Today, I'm really proud of Chris Washburn, or the man he's become, the potential he has showed and for the willingness to tell his truth about where he's been.

"My relationship with him didn't get good until he separated with my mom, and we moved out. I was kinda like, wow! I kinda miss this guy. But also, not living under the same roof with him made it a lot easier for me to want a relationship with him.

"Today, he's the person that I call when I need someone to calm me down. He's the person that I run to when I genuinely need anything. At this point, it's crazy. I'm twenty-five years old, and he's still taking care of me like I'm his little girl."

Former teammates and coaches are happy that Washburn has not only survived but is thriving today.

JOHN LUCAS: "I'm from Raleigh, which is close to Hickory. So, I knew of Chris Washburn and kinda followed him. He would look like he was getting his act together, but then he would regress. I wasn't disappointed because I knew what it took to get healthy. It took me six years to completely stop using drugs once I admitted I had a drug problem. For a long time, I didn't know what I had.

"I'm really proud of Chris Washburn and the man he's become, for the potential he has showed. And for the willingness to tell his truth about where he's been because he may be that the story you and him are writing may be the only big book in the recovery field that helps somebody not go down the same road."

Today, Washburn does not try to look back, but he does have one regret.

CHRIS WASHBURN: "I think maybe not being able to do all the things I wanted to do for my family and others. I am a real big believer in taking care your fellow man. I had that opportunity, and I kinda dropped the ball. That ruined my life. I probably would've taken a different, more constructive path in life. Like I said, I definitely wouldn't have had the same people in my life that I do now."

He says there is one thing he would do differently if he could live his life over.

CHRIS WASHBURN: "A lot of things in my early life were good. I might not have had the kids I have now if I didn't go to that gym that day. I would not have met my first wife Michelle. And if I didn't go to that club that night, I would not have met Monique."

On further reflection, yes, he does have one more regret.

CHRIS WASHBURN: "If I never let Len Bias into my dorm room that night in 1986, I would never have taken my first hit of crack. My life would've probably gone in a totally different direction. But I didn't and it ruined my life. I've owned it and I've survived."

ACKNOWLEDGMENTS

We would like to thank our mutual friend Gregory GL Henderson for bringing us together and helping to jumpstart this project.

We would also like to thank Gregory GL Henderson, along with the following individuals, for the informative interviews that helped to illuminate Chris Washburn's story: Todd Black, Mike Chris, Dee J., Antwoine Higgins, Cliff Levingston, Chris Lightner, Claire Lightner, John Lucas, Ruby McClendon, Bishop McDuffie, Nate McMillan, Ernie Myers, Jessica R., Chris Washburn, Jr., Julian Washburn, Monique Washburn, Montavia Washburn, Marc Washington, Spud Webb, Dereck Whittenburg, Al Young.

Thank you to Chuckie Brown for providing the well-written foreword for this book.

Chris would like to thank the following individuals for their support and friendship during the good times and the bad: Chuckie Brown, Gregory GL Henderson, Patrice Johnson. Jones, Cliff Levingston, Chris Lightner, Claire Lightner, John Lucas, Nate McMillan, Jessica R., Chris Washburn, Jr., Mark Washburn, Monique Washburn, Chri Washburn, Montavia Washburn, Anthony (Spud) Webb, Dereck Whittenburg, Nick Williams, and family.

Chris and Ron would like to thank Jessica R. and the North Carolina State Public Relations Department for providing photos for the book.

Chris would like to give a special thanks to Ron Chepesiuk for his collaboration on this book.

Ron would like to thank Chris Washburn for his collaboration on this book and for sharing his remarkable story. Chris was a generous and exceptional subject.

SOURCES

INTERVIEWS

Todd Black, Mike Chris, Dee J., Gregory G L Henderson, Antoine Higgins, Cliff Levingston, Chris Lightner, Claire Lightner, John Lucas, Ruby McClendon, Bishop McDuffie, Nate McMillan, Ernie Myers, Jessica Riley, Chris Washburn, Jr., Monique Washburn, Montavia Washburn, Spud Webb, Dereck Whittenburg, Al Young

BOOKS

--Hawthorne, Samantha, Goodnight Wolfpack: A Bedtime Story for North Carolina State University. Independently Published, 2022

--Peeler, Tim, and Roger Winstead, NC State Basketball: 100 Years of innovation. University of North Carolina Press, Chapel Hill, NC 2022.

--Walker, J. Samuel, North Carolina State University Men's Basketball Games: A Complete Record, Fall 1953 Through Spring 2006, McFarland and Company, 2008 (News Banks)

ARTICLES (News Banks)

--American News, 193-2024

--NewspaperArchive, 1983 -2024

--Newxspapers.com, 1983-2024

INTERNET

--Addicted to Crack: Basketball Great Chris Washburn Tells His Story. https://www.youtube.com/watch?v=WWBr0IWPBu8

--"Chris Washburn," https://www.youtube.com/watch?v=AGfcgNde7Mc

--Chris Washburn NBA Bust #3 Overall pick in 1986 NBA Draft https://www.youtube.com/watch?v=fAU3-QsWqv0

--Podcast with Chris Washburn on Spud Webb, Nate McMilan, Drugs and more https://www.youtube.com/watch?v=6olzqNmaKew

--WASHED! Top 3 Pick In The Draft! Went To Rehab 14 Times! CHRIS WASHBURN Stunted Growth https://www.youtube.com/watch?v=6YMNz7LX I

For More News About Ron Chepesiuk and Chris Washburn, Signup For Our Newsletter:

http://wbp.bz/newsletter

Word-of-mouth is critical to an author's long-term success. If you appreciated this book please leave a review on the Amazon sales page:

https://wbp.bz/oobreviews

This true crime memoir is both a "high-speed train trip through the modern cocaine trade" and a story of reform, redemption and family (Gerald Posner, and author of *Pharma*).